WE WERE STRANGERS ONCE, TOO

AN IMMIGRANT MEMOIR COLLECTION

EDITED BY SHAWN ADLER

WE WERE STRANGERS ONCE, TOO

To Waltraud Mayer

"Scripture tells us that we shall not oppress a stranger, for we know the heart of a stranger... we are and always will be a nation of immigrants. We were strangers once, too."

—President Barack Obama,
November 20, 2014

CONTENTS

Introduction..XI

PART 1. **SOME KIND OF GOODBYE**   **1**

John Oriundo (Peru)..3

Erika Chicaiza (Ecuador)..7

Ashley Dutan (Ecuador)..9

Gabriel Dada (Nigeria)..13

Rania Elshaer (Palestine)...17

Hibia Rodrigues (Brazil)..19

Maria Almeida (Portugal)..23

Schudejilove Thercy (Haiti)..27

Steven Barrera (El Salvador)..29

Martha Ortiz Vargas (Mexico) 33

Richy Panama (Ecuador) 39

Alanny Sanchez (Dominican Republic)...41

Andres Perez (Venezuela)..45

Victoria Teixeira (Brazil)...47

PART 2. **THE LONG JOURNEY**   **51**

Scarleth Elizabeth Alvarado Moran (Ecuador).................53

Rubi Arana (Ecuador) 57

Ashley Sira Flores (Venezuela) 61

Katherine Martinez (Venezuela) 65

Julian Aguilar (Ecuador) 69

Brenda Hernandez (Honduras) 73

Aly Trejo (Honduras) 75

Jose Matzar (Guatemala) 79

Mishell Chamba Benitez (Ecuador) 83

Kevin Duchitanga (Ecuador) 87

Marielvis Tablante (Venezuela) 91

Jeysi Garcia (Guatemala) 95

Allinson Diaz (Honduras) 97

PART 3. **BETWEEN TWO WORLDS**   **103**

Emilia Santos (Portugal) 105

Beau Ambroise (Malaysia) 115

Josue Soares (Brazil) 117

Angella Charles (Haiti) 121

Maria Quintao (Brazil) 125

David Adelowo (Nigeria) 131

Rafaela Cura (Brazil) 135

Melody Sanchez (Spain) 137

Jennifer Patricio Melquiades (Brazil) 139

Treasure Poole (Haiti) 141

PART 4. **JOURNEY'S END**   **147**
       TO A NEW BEGINNING

Yewande Hamzat (Nigeria) 149

Winiga Batoma (Togo) 153

Kiwendsida Ouedraogo (Burkina Faso) 155

Damian Tamay (Ecuador) 159

Daniella Oyemonlan (Nigeria) 161

Brianna Aguilar (Mexico) 165

Jhon Salazar (Dominican Republic) 169

Haziq Sajjad (Pakistan) 173

Gabriel Do Carmo (Brazil) 177

Xeida Arce (Peru) 181

Jaylene Gonzalez (Puerto Rico) 185

Erick Villacis (Ecuador) 187

Manyama Kehmor Mara (Liberia) 189

Juan Caicedo (Colombia) 191

Michael Adeleke (Nigeria) 195

Saarah Shabazz (Trinidad) 199

William Xiloj (Guatemala) 203

Ferdousi Begum (Bangladesh)..205

Nicole Velez-Ocampo (Ecuador)..207

Khloe Linton (Jamaica and Liberia)..211

Melissa Masache-Ramos (Ecuador)...213

INTRODUCTION

M ANY YEARS LATER, AS she approached what should have been her middle-age, my mother would look back on her own immigrant journey and remember a small doll called Heidi she had to leave behind before coming to America. She loved Heidi, and cared for her, and in the way of small children would hold the doll close to her heart like she was the most important thing in the world.

The doll called Heidi was one of the many stories my family would tell of how they arrived in this country. There was the one about how my grandfather, born in Germany but raised in Coney Island, was buried alive during World War II. With tears in her eyes, my grandmother would sometimes tell the story of how she got sick on the boat ride to this country, and had to trust her children to the care of a total stranger. My mother once said that she knew my grandfather was magic because in their new home he had two boxes, one from which he could pull ice cream, and the other in which he had trapped tiny people who would talk for their amusement. I was born in America, but these immigrant stories and others became my immigrant story, woven together with other threads in a tapestry that became my heritage.

As I approach what should be my own middle-age, however, I realize that I have forgotten many of these memories, particularly in the absence of those who lived them and who might otherwise continue to share.

I must have gone well over a decade since I thought about the story of my mother's doll until, from among over 400 submissions from students all across Newark, I read a story from a Haitian girl named Schudejilove Thercy who wrote about a doll she once loved and held close to her heart, and how she had to leave this doll behind before coming to America.

In that moment, across nearly eighty years and from opposite sides of the planet, I saw my mother's story echoed in someone else's. I became overwhelmed with emotion and felt a sudden and beautiful connectedness that even now is hard to explain.

***

Initial conversions about this book began back in the summer of 2022. At that time, I was working on another collection of student memoirs in cooperation with Ramapo College of New Jersey, a compilation called *The Helpers* which was to be about people who acted as mentors to students, told by the young kids who were helped. We knew we wanted to give the students of

Newark a similar opportunity to showcase their voices, to elevate their stories, and to share their experiences with the world.

As we brainstormed topics, we kept coming back to the idea that it could be a transformative opportunity for empathy to showcase memoirs about the immigrant experience. Ours is an urban community composed mainly of immigrants and other minorities, where many of our students struggle with language barriers, economic instability, and health and safety concerns exacerbated by systemic injustices. Over 90% of our students self-identify as an ethnic minority. A language other than English is spoken in nearly half of all homes.

As adults who care about and work with children, these statistics disguise a deeper truth that goes beyond numbers. As we learn about our students, and share in their hurts and joys, we see individuals who need nurture and care and love, each with their own deeply personal story to share. By listening to these stories, it is the fundamental truth of good teachers that there are no strangers in their classrooms.

The compilation you hold in your hand is composed of 58 such vulnerable and personal stories, representing student experiences from 24 countries, 5 continents, and told in over a dozen unique languages. They were selected from over 400 harrowing and heartbreaking submissions, and have been divided into four chapters organized by theme: narratives about saying goodbye, about the hard and arduous journey to America, about feeling stuck between two cultures, and finally about life in the United States. They were solicited with the cooperation of Newark Public Schools from thousands of invitees, workshopped, edited, and in some cases, revisited as interviews in foreign languages, transcribed and finally translated over the course of nearly an entire year.

During this time, as we told our stories of immigration, narratives of "immigration" once again took center stage in America.

In December 2023, as stories like Schudejilove's started to come in from all across the city, US Customs and Border Protection reported over 250,000 unique encounters with migrants on the US-Mexico border, a number that was notable as the highest ever on record, easily eclipsing the previous high of 224,000. This record influx seemed to convince people on both sides of the political aisle that immigration needed "fixing." According to a poll conducted by the Pew Research Center, 57% of Americans believe in this election year that immigration should be a priority of the President. This number has risen sharply in the last few years, the Center contends, up from 39% at the beginning of Joe Biden's presidency. In February, the same week we invited over one hundred handpicked students from across Newark to improve their stories at an editing day, public and political vitriol came at immigrants from all sides, as a bipartisan attempt to "fix the border crisis" failed to pass the US Senate. Literally yesterday as I write this introduction, former President and current Republican nominee Donald Trump called some migrants "not people" and "animals" and promised, if elected, to have the "largest deportation effort in history."

In response to this hate and misunderstanding, we present a small rebuke: the compilation you hold in your hands. It is composed of 58 vulnerable and personal stories, representing student experiences from 24 countries, 5 continents, and told in over a dozen unique languages.

It is our sincere hope that as you read them, you see your story echoed in the story of someone else, and you feel a sudden and beautiful connectedness that perhaps you find hard to explain.

***

Years later, my grandparents went back to Germany and somehow found my mother's doll. They brought it back to America, and surprised my mother with it on one of her birthdays.

I don't remember my mother doing a lot of creative things when I grew up, but she became possessed by the idea that this story of hers could be a children's book and so wrote it down in the simple, straightforward language of many immigrants for whom English came later. After I read Schudejilove's story I became desperate to read it again, and tore my house apart trying to find it. Many days of panic went by before I found it in a box way in the back of a closet.

My mother died suddenly twenty-five years ago when I was the same age as the children in this collection, before she could publish her book about her doll. Born Waltraud Mayer, she legally changed her first name as an adult, frustrated by a lifetime of encountering people unable to pronounce it. She changed her name again in the book, calling herself Sonya. It ends like this:

"Sonya had the best dream that night. All the little girls in all the world were taking their dolls for a walk together."

Here, finally, is our book, full of all the dreams of all the little girls (and boys) from all the world. Look at how they walk together, one story connecting to the other, each one a small part of a larger American Dream that promises grace to immigrants, that tells us it is impossible to hate when we listen and understand.

Look how they love, and hurt, and in the way of small children, hold their stories close, carrying them around in their hearts like so many tiny, porcelain dolls.

—*Shawn Adler,* March 2024

PART ONE

SOME KIND OF GOODBYE

BUT, SOMETIMES TOO, IN THE STREETS, AND THE HOMES, AND THE LONG DARK HALLWAYS, THE STORY ISN'T JUST ABOUT THE PEOPLE WHO COME, IT'S ABOUT THE TEARS OF THE PEOPLE YOU LEAVE BEHIND.

JOHN ORIUNDO

(PERU)

I T WAS SUMMER WHEN my family started to make arrangements to welcome my uncle and his family. We prepared our basement with beds, a kitchen, and a tiny bathroom - just enough room to fit five people in relative comfort and more than enough for my uncle, my aunt, and their three kids until they got on their feet.

Though their journey was a long one - from Peru, up through South America, over the Mexican desert and across the Rio Grande into Texas - we were granted periodic updates thanks to FaceTime, which my uncle had on his phone.

One night, I was awakened by a loud noise coming from outside my bedroom. Through my door I could see the living room lights on and, though half-asleep, I could hear my dad's voice, loud but not angry. I peeked out, tip-toeing through the hallway to see what the commotion was, careful not to disturb him in my curiosity. He was talking to my cousin.

"*No puedes llevarlo*," he said.

I walked closer. I could now see my cousin was somewhere under a hot sun, his face wet with sweat and tears.

"*No puedes llevarlo*," my father said again.

It took me a while to fully understand what was happening, but, soon, I was able to piece it together from their overheard conversation.

Somewhere, just south of the Rio Grande River, my uncle - on foot with his wife, his two sons, and his four-year-old daughter, years after his brothers had made the dangerous journey, and some months yet before he would finally reach their home in Newark, after careful and meticulous planning, his eyes looking straight ahead past the desert sands and over the swift river and beyond the many generations his children and their children would spend in America - collapsed and died without warning. He was standing. And then, suddenly, he was not.

My cousin, his son, dragged and carried his body over many miles before calling my father.

"*No puedes llevarlo*," my father told him.

Knowing it would be impossible to drag a body over the river and across the border, my dad had to tell his nephew to leave his dead brother's body behind as it would only hold them back.

They left the body with a note and a small cross,

almost 3,000 miles from my uncle's home in Peru, and not quite a dozen or so miles from their goal. In a few days, they knew the body would be gone, eviscerated by animals or the weather.

In the weeks that followed, I began to see my dad less and less. He would be in the basement, alone, quiet, television playing in the background. I'd sometimes bring down food for him, but he'd just let the plates stack up, overflowing with food from previously untouched meals. He would come home from work, shower, and sit for the rest of the day.

Months passed and his family finally made it to New Jersey. A van was parked outside my house, and one by one they all stepped outside. We welcomed them - everyone except the person my dad most wanted to see.

The next day, I gathered the courage to ask my dad, "*¿Todo bien?*" I felt stupid asking him how he was doing, knowing full well the choice he had made and the depression it caused, but I didn't know what else to say. He looked at me. He smiled and caressed my hair. His face said it all. I hugged him, and I could feel tears hit my shoulder. Being the head of our family had put so much pressure on him. I knew how much it meant to him that we are all safe.

He pulled back and just nodded yes. I smiled a little and said "okay."

"*No puedes llevarlo,*" I told him. "You cannot carry it."

"Not alone."

ERIKA CHICAIZA

(ECUADOR)

T HE DAY I FOUND out I was coming to the United States, it was very difficult for me to accept because I had a little dog. He was my whole life, and I didn't know who to leave him with since no one was going to take care of him like me.

He was such a little dog.

My brother found him abandoned on the streets with very dirty and long fur. We were very sad to see him like this so we brought him home and fed him and gave him water. The next day we took him to a dog groomer who could give him a bath and a haircut. He was so scared those first few days, but eventually he learned to love us and our house. In the mornings, when they opened the door for him to enter the house, he would come running to find me in bed and wake me up.

He was a very happy dog. He liked to jump and play with his stuffed animal and sleep with me.

When they told me that we were going to America, I tried to spend the most beautiful moments with him. My mother had already planned who she was going to leave him with, so we knew he would be cared for, but as the day of departure got closer, I became sadder and sadder. Finally, the day arrived. In the morning we had our last meal together, and then I went to pick up his things: his plate, food, and toys.

We put his leash on and went to take the bus. I think he thought that it was a normal walk like always. But when we hugged him goodbye and walked away, we could see the lady had already tied him up to a post. He looked scared because he didn't know what was happening.

I knew I would never see him again.

And so I looked back at my dog—I looked back at my dog and said goodbye to him forever.

ASHLEY DUTAN

(ECUADOR)

M Y MOTHER HAD JUST turned 19 when dreams of America became too powerful to sleep on any longer. By this time, both my grandfather and father had been in the United States for over a year and were regularly sending money back to their family still in Ecuador.

"Come to the United States," my grandfather told her. "Here is where women get opportunities to work."

My mother was a foolish person and so this promise of opportunity spoke to her. She came from a humble background, spending her childhood in a home she shared with nine other people; at times struggling to afford food, so poor she would sometimes eat the weeds. She dreamed, instead, of cakes and riches and the chance to be happy. But most of all, she dreamed of a house; a home where her six month old daughter, my sister Jessica, could have her own room.

My grandmother begged my mother to think of her newborn child and stay in Ecuador. My father, who had already made the perilous journey across land and water to America, pleaded with her to do the same. This only made my mother more resolute. Everyone doubted that my fragile mother could make it all the way to the United States on her own, but the chances would be zero, they argued, with a child not yet weaned. Pressure mounting from all sides, my mother was finally inspired to make a concession and so, with tears in her heart, she agreed to leave her baby daughter in the care of her grandmother. Not long after, she left her hometown of Cuenca and started to hitchhike the way to Guayaquil. Subsequently, she traveled on a boat for seven days towards Guatemala, and then boarded a fishing boat towards Mexico.

As my mother traveled to the US, she was able to form a group with other travelers on the road to America. Eventually, they had to cross a giant river, and so began to make preparations. Some in her group discovered logs while others opted for tires. My mother grabbed empty water bottles and used them as a method of staying afloat. Even with all this preparation, no one could anticipate the river's riptides, and soon my mother was bobbing dangerously below the water. She couldn't tell whether she was going to live or die. She considered letting the river take her.

"What are you doing? We made it here, are you trying to make it all go to waste?" she heard a man yell, and the urge to live overwhelmed her. She grabbed his hand and was pulled to safety on the opposite shore.

Meanwhile, my sister grabbed someone else's hand. She crawled. She babbled. She grew.

***

My mother found herself in a land where she didn't know the way. She walked and walked for thousands of miles until she met up with my father again in New Jersey. Yet, when she finally arrived, she couldn't adapt. She would feign that she was alright, yet wouldn't eat properly for years, wracked with guilt over abandoning her child so many thousands of miles away. She knew that both of them would have died in the river crossing - she wasn't completely naive - but her thoughts were still full of Jessica.

For years after she would try to reconnect, but their relationship never healed. Jessica didn't know who she was or why this strange woman kept calling. Once she was old enough to comprehend who our mother was, she was angry. She would go years cutting off contact completely.

She is 27 years old today, and it has been 26 years since my mother last saw her. There is no doubt in my mind that she rightfully harbors resentment towards us. Jessica is a mother of three kids now, married with a job as a teacher. She's made a life without me in it and I can't bear to intrude.

***

Originally, my mother aspired to achieve financial prosperity. However, she has since shared that she has a new dream: She wants her children - all her children - to become successful.

But I know better. Late at night she closes her eyes and dreams nothing of success. She dreams of Ecuador. She dreams of her old house and her grandfather and the dirt floor.

She dreams of holding her daughter one more time and never letting go.

GABRIEL DADA

(NIGERIA)

G ROWING UP, I NEVER thought my father felt like we were good enough for him. He was born into a big family in Nigeria- the fifth of nine children. But his own kids always felt like an afterthought.

One day, early in his life, back when he brushed his teeth with mint leaves and walked miles for a bucket of water, my dad was sent on an errand with his younger two siblings. They were twins. He was supposed to bring them to school and then he would go to work (he himself had dropped out of school to help with the bills). As my father and his siblings were riding the bus, he heard gunshots. He saw people dressed up as soldiers, bandanas on their heads. My father immediately panicked because he knew exactly who these people were - they were Boko Haram, terrorists in Nigeria who kidnapped others to hold them for ransom. My father hurriedly told my siblings to hide but it was too late, the Boko Haram took everyone out of the bus and covered their heads with black bags.

My father woke up in a pitch black room unable to see. He called out in the darkness for his siblings until, finally, he heard his brother call out in response. He rushed to them and found them sitting in a corner scared to death with tears rolling down their cheeks. He gave them both a big hug to try to calm them down.

As they were hugging, Boko Haram soldiers entered the room and told everyone to get in a single file line. One by one they were told to call their loved ones to pay for their ransom. All was going well until one person's family wasn't able to pay the ransom of 1 million Naira (about $1000). That was when chaos started. The soldier pulled out his gun and shot the person.

My father's younger siblings couldn't take it anymore. They started crying for their mother and father. My dad hurriedly shushed them but to no avail: the Boko Haram soldier heard the cries and smiled as he looked at my father's two siblings. He shouted for my father and his siblings to come to the front of the line. There my father had to ask his parents for 3 million Naira for the release of them all. Instead, they started shouting and crying. They told him that they only had enough for one person.

The soldier began to laugh. He grabbed my father's little brother and sister and left the room. My father screamed for them to stop but he couldn't do anything. The soldier had a gun and he didn't.

For days and days my father begged for knowledge of what happened to his brother and sister, but he never saw them again after that. After a month my father was released. When his parents saw him they couldn't even recognize him. They say he changed. Eventually, he left Nigeria, making his way to the United States in hopes of creating a better life, far away from the memory of violence.

After my father and mother divorced, I hated him. At his worst, he was cruel to her and to us. At his best, I still never felt like he chose us, or wanted us, or loved us. As the years went by, I could not find it in my heart to forgive him. Sometimes, he just doesn't feel like he's here.

And sometimes, now, my father reaches out in the dark but there is nobody left to reply.

RANIA ELSHAER

(PALESTINE)

S HIFA ELSHARKAWY, MY GREAT-GRANDMOTHER, was the first person in my family to be forced out of Palestine.

Born and raised in Yibna, she was caught up in the Arab-Israeli War of 1948 and the subsequent displacement known as Nabka, or the "catastrophe." Forced to leave her home and all of her belongings she walked many miles, carrying her siblings on her back, until she eventually reached Majdal Asqalan on the Egyptian border and then Gaza, where she boarded a train with promises to return.

At fourteen, she had to provide for her family as the primary source of income and so became a seamstress. Soon, she got married and, not long after, had my grand-mother, Asma - all desperate, in some way, to return home.

Handuma El Aga and her son, Talaat Elashkar, my grandfather, were the second and third people in my family to be forced to leave Palestine, on a train to a small village called Elsharkaya, Egypt. Talaat was forced to leave his school at the age of ten because his father had passed away, and he went to work to provide for his five siblings. Talaat soon married Asma and, together, they had Alyaa Elashkar, my mother, who was born and raised in Egypt but knew from birth that she was Palestinian, a fact made doubly real because Egypt refused to grant any of them citizenship.

It took 75 years, but the last of my family was finally forced to leave Palestine, this time in body bags. A few months ago, every cousin still left was killed when a missile hit their home.. There is no one left to leave because there is no one left.

My mother and father never knew Palestine as a physical place, but only an idea. They moved further away, to America, where I have grown - attached to a land I've never been to and never seen, destined from birth to have left a place to which I can never return.

HIBIA RODRIGUES

(BRAZIL)

THE PERIOD WHEN MY mother was pregnant with me was a difficult time for her, as her health had been unstable since her own childhood, and her lungs didn't function well.

My mother was a strong, organized, and very dedicated woman who fought for everything she wanted, and always tried to provide the best for me and my sister. But her poor health meant that there was only so much she could do, especially since my father had left some years prior to go to America. During this time, my mother worked at a woman's house taking care of her children, and studying nursing. Sometimes, my mother had to stay late at her boss's house, and I had to take care of my sister. Occasionally, she took us to our aunt's house because she couldn't come home at all.

Eventually, given her health, my father decided to bring us to the United States, and my mother agreed.

She sold our wardrobes, clothes, sofa, beds - anything she could get a fair dollar for - and gave away what was left to her sisters. When everything was ready, and the day of our departure arrived, I was nervous and scared because I didn't understand much, but my mother said it was ok, that it was the three of us and God.

We took God with us on a very long journey.

For a long time, we were stuck in Mexico; first at a hotel, and then at a strange man's house. It was here that, after many hundreds of miles, we were able to shower, eat, and rest. Despite this, my mother struggled, her health deteriorating.

When it was our turn to leave, we boarded a bus to the border, but it wasn't long before the bus was stopped, and some people were asked to get off. I was nervous, but my mother told me to stay calm and to say nothing. The officer interrogated my mother, asking if I was really her daughter. Then the officer asked me if my mother was really my mother. I looked at him and said yes.

"What's her favorite color?"

"My mother doesn't have a favorite color. She loves all the colors and doesn't have a favorite."

Many people were not allowed to go further.

Soon, we reached immigration, where we were held. There was a huge line of people surrendering, and the officers checked us. When it was our turn to be taken, they put us in a car with bars and transferred us to a fenced location.

My mother laid towels on the floor and covered us with the aluminum foil blankets they had given us to keep warm.

We were hungry and thirsty and felt sick. But, like always, my mother bore the worst of it. It was here in the immigration facility, and more broadly in America, that she started to get really ill.

My mother had been sick since childhood, but worsened in the United States after migrating without rest across many countries in such cramped and squalid conditions. From that time on, she was always in the hospital. Soon, she couldn't breathe on her own and needed a special machine. Every night, I slept unwell, worried and afraid that the machine would stop working and I would wake up to find my mother dead next to me.

Soon, she couldn't even eat soft foods. And then there came a day when she was hospitalized and never came back home at all.

On the last day of her life, my father took us to the hospital, and when I arrived, I saw her connected to several machines, tubes coming out of her face. The doctors said I couldn't touch her, that nothing I could do would help, but I started touching and calling to her anyway, hoping she would open her eyes and call me by my name.

When she died, we sent her body back to Brazil.

On the car ride home from the hospital, I thought about my sister and my father, and how we would now be making the next journey together - the three of us and God. It was raining, and tears fell down my face when I noticed a rainbow. I looked at it in wonder. I remembered my mother raising us in Brazil, working all those jobs and staying late all those nights. I could see our long journey to America - how tired we were and hungry and scared - and how my mom kept us going, how she made it all the way to the end before collapsing.

Then, suddenly, there in the car, looking at the rainbow, I remembered my mother saying she loved all the colors and didn't have a favorite.

MARIA ALMEIDA

(PORTUGAL)

U NTIL I TURNED NINE, I lived in Portugal and maintained a close relationship with my father, despite my parents' separation. My visits to his place were always enjoyable, and his girlfriend treated me like her own daughter. I was a daddy's girl, and loved the way it felt to be loved by him.

The situation worsened when my mom made the decision to move to America. I wasn't ready to say goodbye to my father, and to our regular visits, and to the ways in which I identified myself through my love for him. Deep down, I knew this last visit would be significant, and wanted the goodbye to be something I could always remember.

It had been a while since our last visit and my dad looked me up and down while I stood in the doorway.

"*As tuas maminhas já estão a crescer*," he joked.

I let out an awkward laugh because his talking about my appearance made me uncomfortable. My mom quickly and politely changed the subject. She told me to give him a hug and say goodbye.

Back home, her politnesses receded. Unable to hold it in any longer, my mother erupted, her words bouncing off the walls as she aggressively stacked dishes in the sink.

"I told you to stop giving your father the benefit of the doubt," she yelled. "All he does is disappoint you. Then I'm the one who has to hear about it!"

Her eyes were kind, but the words she wanted to land softly pierced my heart instead. Her shoulders dropped. "He doesn't know how to be a father," she said. "All he does is hurt you."

I tried to respond, to tell her that he was my father and I would love him no matter what. But the words got caught in my throat and I couldn't finish the sentence.

Months later, we finally arrived in America. I eagerly awaited a call from my father to share the excitement of our first day, to tell him the story of our flight and arrival through customs - but no call came. It was three weeks later when my mother handed me the phone.

"Now he remembers he has a daughter," she sarcastically said, tossing me the line.

It was his wife. A miracle, she said - a thing thought impossible. She was pregnant and my father was going to be a dad.

As much as I wanted to be an older sister, I couldn't help but wonder what this would mean for our relationship. He didn't even have the courage to deliver the news himself, but had relegated the responsibility to his wife while he stood behind her in shadow. It became clear that he was starting a new family in France and was leaving me behind.

Going to be a dad, she had said.

From that point on, my father and I would go months without speaking, until one day, we stopped speaking altogether.

Some days I think about the conversation I had with my mother the day I last saw him. She told me that day he didn't know how to be a father, and all he did was disappoint me. I think, now, about the days in Portugal when I was daddy's girl, and I think about how much I loved the feeling of being loved by him.

I think about how I promised that day to love him no matter what.

SCHUDEJILOVE THERCY

(HAITI)

When I was a little girl I had a toy doll with beautiful hair, which I loved to comb over and over again. I couldn't go anywhere without my doll.

The doll was such a beautiful doll and special in a way I couldn't understand as a child, because it reminded me of my baby sister who passed away when she was only six months old.

I was heartbroken when she died.

I remember where I was when I heard the news; and I remember my legs shook and turned to jelly underneath me, and that I was unable to move. I clutched my doll and sat in silence and, from that moment on, couldn't bear to separate myself from her, even for a second. When she would be taken away it was like my soul was being broken, and I would find it hard to breathe.

One day, I got worried I would forget my little sister and started to cry, but holding my doll I felt better. I knew

I could remember her when I held my doll, and so the doll became my blood, and my heart, and my life, and my sister's love. Even though she is not here I miss her every day and every second, and I will always hurt, I thought. But I hurt a little less when I had my doll.

Eventually, my parents decided that for my well-being and my health it was better to take the doll.

"*Sè ou nan yon pi bon kote, mwen konnen li fè mal men ou dwe kontinye ak lavi ou,*" my mother said, a lone tear dropping down her face and marking her red, cotton dress.

"*Schude,*" my father gently said, wrapping his lean arm around me and sighing, "*Schudenika ap toujou nan kè nou, men li lè pou nou kite ale. Ou dwe debarasse de poupe ou. Li lè.*"

"But where is Schudenika?" I kept repeating, tears falling down my face uncontrollably, my whole body shaking as I gripped the doll tightly. I always asked where my little sister was when the doll was not with me.

They took the doll from me that day and buried her in a secret place in Haiti I know not where, and there she lies waiting for me to grow up, and leave America, and come back - waiting after all these years for me to come find her.

STEVEN BARRERA

(EL SALVADOR)

WHEN I LIVED IN El Salvador I used to love going fishing with my grandfather out on the river, where the blue went deeper and further than you could imagine. I loved spending time with my grandfather, my cousins and family.

It was while I was at my grandparents that I learned my brother had been kidnapped from university. I was only nine-years-old and not aware of everything that was happening, but I saw my mother crying, desperate for his safety. Criminals had captured and tortured him, and promised his safe return only after a sizable ransom had been paid. They sent a photo of my brother with a gun to his head as proof.

My mother had to sell some land in order to negotiate his return.

When we finally saw my brother, he was beaten up pretty bad, his face swollen - but he was alive. It was shortly after that my mother told us we were moving to America.

On the road to the United States, we crossed many waters. Sometimes, we slept on the sides of creeks, outside on ranches, hungry from lack of food. Sometimes, we would watch as the coyotes threw our money at police to ensure we could forge a stream. Sometimes we enjoyed the journey precisely because it was a winding path like a river, and at night the coyotes would let us rest and make tacos. Sometimes we had to walk very long roads out of our way, digging footprints deep in the sand like canals, so the *Migra* would not find us.

When we arrived in Mexico, they locked us in a house for about a week but eventually we headed to the last big river: the Rio Grande. When we reached the bank, the coyotes made us throw away all our clothes, and give them all our money and valuables, since they told us on the other side immigration would take everything and give nothing back. One by one we got in an inflatable raft, until all twelve of us were squeezed together, packed like fish in a tin. Underneath, an additional person would hold his breath and push up the raft from the bottom so we didn't drown. It felt at every second like the raft was going to sink because there were so many people in it, and I was very scared because I couldn't swim. I remember at that moment my brother holding me, helping me to the other side.

We found *La Migra*, and I was separated from my family. They put me in the ice box with the other minors and gave me an apple. Ten days later, they let us bathe and sent us to Newark.

America was supposed to be the place where we would be free from the dangers of home. We had traveled thousands of miles for my brother's safety but it was in New Jersey, not El Salvidor, where they found his dead, swollen body. We do not know his cause of death, or what happened, or why he died the way he did.

We know only that we live by another ocean now. We know the waters are blue and deep and vast and, one day, the waters that chart our lives will cover everything and everyone, the living and the dead.

MARTHA ORTIZ VARGAS

(MEXICO)

It was planting day at the farm and I could see that the effort would bring about a good harvest. The fresh wind crossed my face and the sun was hiding behind the mountains, when I felt a hand touch my shoulder and heard a voice that I had known for a long time.

"I love you very much. Never forget it."

I turned around and looked at my father smiling behind me.

That day we were at my grandparents, and I got distracted playing with my cousins. When I came back to the house I discovered that my mom, dad, and little brother had left without me. I thought nothing of it, and figured they would come back for me later. Soon, though, I heard my aunt getting her car keys.

"Go in the room with your cousins," she said. "I'll be back."

Her face had no color and her voice trembled. I felt uneasy, but I couldn't connect the dots before a wailing came from the other room.

"They killed him," my grandfather shouted. "They killed my son."

When we arrived at the scene of the murder, the first thing I noticed was my dad's motorcycle, then an ambulance, then the screams of my little brother, his mouth full of blood, my mother on her knees trying to stop the life that was pouring out of my father's head. I walked closer to help her, but the only thing I can remember was the voice of one of my cousins.

"*Titi*," he said. "I can't stop the bleeding, I cover one side and the blood comes out through the other."

I wanted to run to my father, but the paramedics were pushing me away while lifting him inside the ambulance. The bullet had impacted his forehead and the pressure of the stoppage made his body swell to such a point that it seemed as if he was going to explode. Miraculously, he was still breathing, but each labored breath he took felt like the wind was sucked out of my lungs - like I was dying too.

My little brother couldn't stop crying. And somewhere in the madness, my older sister arrived to find us covered in our father's blood. She took us back to our grandparents'. We prayed.

Many hours later my father's body finally arrived at my grandmother's house where we held the viewing. The house was bursting with kind people who knew him and the wonderful person he was. Saying goodbye to my father was the hardest thing I had to do in my life, but it was comforting to be surrounded by so many people and so much love.

In Mexico, there is love almost everywhere. But in those places where love cannot reach - the dark and the violent places - the Cartel sneaks in.

***

Losing my father was an unbearable pain, but what I didn't know was that my real struggle in life was just beginning. Two weeks after my father's murder, I had my elementary school graduation. At that moment, I couldn't hold myself together. My vision was blurred by the tears coming down my face and I collapsed on the floor. The first thing I remember after coming to my senses was my mother telling us we would have to flee.

The night before my father was shot, his cousin's husband became violent, and hit his wife. My father could no longer stand to see this happen to someone he loved, and so he took his cousin and her children away to hide them from the monster they lived with. At that time this man was very powerful within the Cartel, and the next day, feeling wronged, he killed my father for standing up to him. Soon, my mother began to receive many letters

- threatening letters - telling her to drop the charges and refuse to testify - or else.

My mother would not be intimidated, but the reality was our whole family had targets on our backs and, because of these threats, we were forced to relocate. I spent all of this period in deep grief, often alone, locked up in my room, refusing food for many days to the point of physical and mental exhaustion. The depression I felt was so enormous that I couldn't see beyond the cage I was trapped in.

In total, we were out of our home for two years, sometimes together, sometimes split up. My mother would come to see us every time she could, but no matter where we were, the Cartel would find us. My home vanished along with my father, and the emptiness it left was filled with unease. No matter where we went, we were not safe.

Finally, after three long and violent years on the run, the man who murdered my father was sentenced to 30 years in prison. Still, some threats persisted. Relocating was devastating and exhausting, running from one place to another trying to hide and, so, in the end, my mother decided to stop running altogether and apply for political asylum in the United States. Not long after, we were able to start fresh in a new home.

The road was long and scary and full of danger, but I believe that because my father stood up for what was right, all his children are now all safe - far away from

Mexico and the Cartel and the fields where long ago good seeds were planted to grow strong crops.

I remember that on the day my father was murdered my mother called from the hospital. Somehow he was still alive, his heart refusing to give in. She held the receiver to his ears and told us to say goodbye. Through the phone I could hear her whisper.

"*No te preocupes viejo*," she said to him. "*Yo los voy a cuidar bien*."

On the phone, my mother spoke to us now.

She told us our father loved us very much. She told us to never forget it.

RICHY PANAMA

(ECUADOR)

M Y MOST BELOVED MEMENTO is a hand bracelet. I got this bracelet from my father, which is very important to me, since it makes me think about him. He is so far away and looking at it makes me feel that he is close.

When we separated, my dad held the bracelet in his hand.

"*Este, Richy, es un regalo muy especial,*" he told me. "*porque mi padre me lo dio y ahora te lo doy a ti.*"

I felt the weight of the bracelet when I grabbed it. My grandfather had passed it down to my father, and now I was the third person in my family to have it. I looked at it with awe.

"*Gracias, papá, por esto,*" I said. "*Me encanta porque siempre te sentiré cerca. Muchísimas gracias. Me encanta.*"

I held the silver bracelet in my hand and it turned from cold to warm as my grip tightened. Finally, I placed the bracelet on my wrist and felt it move up and down.

My father is very far away from me because he is in Ecuador and I am in the United States. He does not have a visa and cannot be here himself. But every time I have fear or anxiety or feel alone, I look at the bracelet on my hand and I feel that he is by my side. It makes me feel like I am strong and brave, like him.

It is a small thing, and may not seem important to other people, even something without any value, but for me this bracelet does more than wrap around my wrist. This very special bracelet wraps around the whole world.

ALANNY SANCHEZ

(DOMINICAN REPUBLIC)

NICOLE DIED WHEN WE were seven. Despite her age, her death wasn't unexpected. She had cancer and her mom was too poor to afford proper treatment.

We lived in a small village in the fields of the Dominican Republic, far up on some mountains. Our village was surrounded by acres and acres of mango and cherry trees. Deep in the woods, there was a calm, clear river. We used to spend all our afternoons there before Nicole got sick. If we weren't climbing trees and picking fruits, we were jumping fully clothed into the river from the rocks above. We'd walk home soaked and inevitably get sound spankings, but that never deterred us from doing it time and time again.

When Nicole got sick, she couldn't go out anymore, but I'd visit her almost daily. We'd spend our afternoons in her house playing with Barbies and painting with watercolors. Her mom would sit on a chair in the corner with a tissue always in hand and watch us as we played. Sometimes she'd whisper to us in a strained voice to not make a mess out of the paint, but that was as much as we ever talked.

One day when I visited Nicole, all her hair had disappeared. I burst into tears on the spot. She too began sobbing, calling herself ugly.

After that day, Nicole stopped visiting.

Once, during a storm, when all the kids were playing in the rain and rolling around in mud, I saw Nicole again. She came running towards me, her face lit up with a wide smile. Guilt filled me and I immediately ran home. When the rain stopped, I went outside to play in the mud some more, but there she was. Crouched down with her knees tucked into her chest, she was drawing flower patterns on the tracks of mud I left on the porch when I ran home. She looked up at me and smiled, but all I could see was her hairless scalp. She wasn't supposed to be outside, so when my grandma saw her crouched on our porch she immediately called for Nicole's mom. Her mom rushed down in a panic to collect her.

Before Nicole died, I visited her once more. She was unconscious. She was laid in her bed, typically a mess, but now neatly made with her tucked in. Her mom was sitting beside her, her big hand wrapped around Nicole's.

The day Nicole passed away, I was outside playing dolls with my cousins. It was very hot. Sweat was trickling all over our faces but we continued playing in the blazing sun. The only thing that stopped us was the scream that reverberated through the whole village. It came from Nicole's house so we didn't have to ask who it was or why it was so loud. We all knew. My throat tightened and my bottom lip started quivering. I dropped my dolls and ran home, hiding under my grandma's bed.

Nicole was buried in a pink fluffy dress, a matching headband around her head. She was laid in a small, white and silver casket. Everything contrasted her dark, dull skin. I was only allowed to see her at the viewing, since my grandma firmly believed that burials weren't for children to watch.

Shortly after, I moved from my quaint and peaceful home deep in the mountains of the Dominican Republic to the bustling city of Newark, New Jersey. I've lived in America now for many years, far from the mountains and the cherry trees and the calm, clear rivers that make their quiet way through forests.

Recently, I realized I could no longer remember Nicole's face. Instead, when I close my eyes I see her sitting, her face down, drawing flower patterns in the mud, her head buried under blankets in a room and a home and a town I can barely recall, above me in a mango tree, her face looking up towards heaven, reaching for a fruit she will never get.

ANDRES PEREZ

(VENEZUELA)

"*¡Vamos a irnos de vacaciones!*" my mother exclaimed, joy and excitement in her voice.

"*¡En serio!*" I screamed with enthusiasm. We hadn't been on a vacation since I was in the second grade, when we visited our family in the United States. I loved it in America and was excited to go back. Everything about it made me happy.

My mother helped me pack.

"*Mete en esta maleta lo que quieras llevarte. Elige bien,*" she said, admonishing me to choose wisely. By the time we finished putting the last item in, we had four suitcases between us - an awful lot compared to my memory of the last time we visited, but enough, I reasoned, for what was sure to be a long trip full of fun.

Two days before we left, it was my ninth birthday. My parents made sure to go big. I remember that my two best friends came over, along with all of my family.

I had never had a birthday party like this before, and I enjoyed every second.

The next day we celebrated another member of my family - my cousin - who was graduating from high school. He was the first one among my generation of cousins to have a graduation, and it was very emotional. My mom cried and gave lots of hugs, holding onto her family tight.

Finally, it was the day of our vacation! We woke up earlier than usual to go to the airport and, not long after, we were in America.

That night my parents sat me down.

"*Te tenemos que decir algo,*" my dad said. "We are not going back home."

For a couple days after, I was still able to convince myself that this was a vacation. Within a couple weeks, I began to feel deceived. And hurt. It was meant to be a short trip and became a lifetime. Today, I wonder if I will ever see my family and friends again.

In a world full of goodbyes, I never got to say mine.

VICTORIA TEIXEIRA

(BRAZIL)

THE FIRST TIME I met my grandfather, he started crying as soon as he saw me.

I remember he showed me a *peteca*. My mother used to play with it on the streets of Brazil when she was my age. Kids in my city didn't play on the streets - sometimes at the park but never on the road where cars would pass. I learned another thing they did was pick fruits right off a tree and eat it. I had never seen a fruit tree in America before. All the kids did that - they would pick the fruit right off the tree. I thought that was so weird.

Soon I had to leave my grandfather and go to my aunt's house. My mom had nine siblings, and out of the nine, I knew she really wanted me to meet her eldest sister the most. She and my mother were very close. In her house, I saw the pictures my mother would send her sister and her father. In one particular picture, I recognized myself as a baby. My aunt showed me my mother's handwriting on the back - light, looping, slanted writing I was not used to.

"*Esta é a minha filha Victoria, eu não sabia que eu podia amar uma pessoa tanto quanto eu amo ela! Eu sinto muita falta de você, minha irmã; principalmente nos finais de semana quando eu me lembro dos passeios que a gente fazia.*"

I walked from house to house among the village. Everywhere I went, each time I was put in front of someone new, they would cry when they saw me. I didn't know if that was good or bad. I remember one corridor in particular, and at the end was a woman who looked older than my mother but a lot like her. I was told she was my mother's sister, and as she picked me up I remember her cry felt worse, the sobbing kind of cry that shakes the body as the tears fell down her face. I remember feeling bad but knowing that there was nothing I could do. I didn't even know why she was crying. My dad and I stayed there for a few more days before it was time to go home.

I've always been told that I looked like my father, as my mother had curly hair and black eyes, while my father and I have straight hair and brown eyes. Nobody in America would ever say that my mother and I looked alike, but it was all I heard in Brazil - something I made sure to tell her when she met us at the airport.

My mother had left her home six years previously, and in all the time since and not seen her father, or sisters. As an undocumented immigrant, she had not dared go back, for fear she wouldn't be able to make the return trip to America. That was her choice, and like many immigrants, her story continued in a new country with a new generation full of new hope, playing new games - taking new photographs. Many times, the story ends there.

But, sometimes too, in the streets, and the homes, and the long dark hallways, the story isn't just about the people who come, it's about the tears of the people you leave behind.

PART TWO

THE LONG JOURNEY

I WILL GO SLOWLY. AND DELIBERATELY. AND EACH DAY I WILL MAKE SURE TO ALWAYS WALK ONE FOOT IN FRONT OF THE OTHER, DIRECTLY STRAIGHT AHEAD.

SCARLETH ELIZABETH ALVARADO MORAN

(ECUADOR)

I T WAS A CRISP fall night and my aunt came to inform my father of terrible news about a shooting involving a close friend, David Andrade, a well-known musician in our canton of El Triunfo. He had been meeting with friends when two vehicles arrived and opened fire with rifles. Desperate, my father rushed on his motorcycle to see what had happened, hoping it was only minor, but upon arriving at the hospital, he was devastated to learn that his friend had died. My father, heartbroken, called my mother to inform her of David's death and that of three others who were with him. This event dramatically changed our family and those close to us; my mother was pregnant with twins and lost the babies due to the shock of what was happening.

From that moment on, my parents decided to not leave the house unless it was an emergency.

Two months passed and another person known to us, Don Juan Sicha, was killed on December 24, shot in the head while driving his vehicle home after dropping off his daughter. He was being extorted and could not or would not pay. Hearing this news I was terrified, especially since my parents also owned a store and were being extorted for monthly payments. Out of fear, my mother temporarily closed the store.

In the following months, a neighbor from our community, Mr. Henry Chele, was also murdered, reigniting fear and terror in our canton. He was a well-known taxi driver and entertainer. While working as a taxi driver, two individuals on a motorcycle shot him dead for refusing to work with the mafia. This event scared us, as young boys from our neighborhood aged 12 to 14 were being recruited by these gangs, leaving their parents powerless to intervene.

Not even a full year after the first murder, my father's cousin, Mr. Ariel Burgos, was gunned down. Apparently, gang members wanted him to commit crimes with them and threatened to kill his father and son if he refused. Despite initially complying, he decided to withdraw from the criminal life, which led to his being followed and ultimately shot multiple times.

Then, what we feared the most happened.

One morning, my parents were at their store when men dressed in black came to the shop. My parents were threatened by these individuals, who claimed to represent "the boss." They were told they had to comply or else the gang would kill their family. My parents knew the police would do nothing.

Alone and unseen by my parents, I cried, afraid of what would happen, but certain in the knowledge that whatever dangers lay ahead, they were nothing compared to the dangers that surrounded us.

That night, I helped my father get our passports ready.

RUBI ARANA

(ECUADOR)

THE WEIGHT OF THE silence was too much to bear.

"They want to kill me," my dad finally said. "We leave now."

We had just settled down in a new house in Ecuador, far from the problems which had plagued my father. We had even bought a new puppy to celebrate our new lives, a dog we named Valentina. It didn't matter. As if the words themselves were not enough, I could see the fear and desperation in my father's eyes. There could be no room for discussion.

"Mija," he pleaded. *"Nos tenemos que ir a los Estados Unidos por nuestra propia seguridad."*

He looked down, suddenly unable to meet my eyes, and told me to pack a single suitcase - warning me only to put in necessary items as whatever couldn't fit would have to be left behind.

"*Solo lo necesario mija nada de porquerías de juguetes o cosas innecesarias.*"

My hands trembled and my heart pounded as I looked around my room for what seemed necessary, knowing my current life and all I had ever known was beginning to slip away.

The first thing I took was a picture of my family from a day we spent at the beach. I took it out of the frame. I was around four years old in the picture, but I remembered vividly that that was the day I learned to swim. More than anything, I wanted a reminder of the happiest moments we experienced in Ecuador as a family - moments that may never happen again and smiles that may never be as bright in the life that awaited us. I put it gently at the bottom of the suitcase.

The next thing I grabbed was a fairytale book, specifically one about princesses. It was my favorite bedtime story. My mom read it to me every night but I never got tired of it. The book and I had been through tough times together - nights I had cried because I had been scared of the dark. But the book had also seen every time my mom kissed me good night.

"*Que sueñes con los angelitos,*" she would say. "Sweet dreams."

A pair of black platform glitter boots that my grandma had brought for me was what I added next. I remembered the argument my mother and I had about whether I could get those shoes or not. I remember being so angry I thought I would burst.

Most of all I packed clothes, regular clothes. I packed shirts, sweaters, and shoes. I packed pants. I packed the white dress I wore to my mother's master's degree graduation. It was the only dress I took because I knew that it was a dress I wore on a day that I could not have been more proud to be her daughter and clap for her as she received her degree. Even if my mom could not use her master's in the United States, I thought, maybe, it could be an example for me to never stop working towards my ambitions.

I couldn't pack our new dog.

I zipped the suitcase and walked outside my bedroom. Everything suddenly felt real, and I knew I would have to leave not just my material possessions, but emotional connections and relationships. My parents were still sitting at the dining room table, with their heads in their hands.

"Mami, Papi," I said. *"No se preocupen verán que ya todo va a estar bien y tal vez, hasta nos vaya mejor allá."*

But it was already too late. It was time. I went to grab my suitcase but the weight of it was too much to bear.

ASHLEY SIRA FLORES

(VENEZUELA)

I N THE JUNGLE, THE people who die die from starvation. Between Venezuela and the United States, there is freedom, but on the road there, between Colombia and Panama, lies the Darien Gap, an ancient jungle thought functionally impassable as recently as a decade ago. Most migrants take a boat around. But since 2010 it is estimated that over 130,000 have traveled through the impossibly dense landscape, many Venezuelan like me.

We spent three days in the jungle, and in that time we saw lots of different people from many different countries - children and pregnant women and the elderly. First, we passed a mountain that was very steep with terrible mud in many places that came to our knees, making climbing nearly impossible. Our guide was always in front, hacking his way through foliage with dual machetes, one in each arm, slicing vines and bushes with skill and speed. We wore boots so that our feet would not falter, knowing a twisted ankle or broken bone would be a death sentence. We were desperate to be out of the jungle, but the motivation to keep moving was all around us, on the ground and in the weeds, where dead bodies were abandoned, sheets over fresh corpses that would become old bones. People unable to go forward would be left. Alone, and unable to move, they would die in the jungle from starvation. At the entrance to the Darien Gap, we saw an old lady in a wheelchair pushed by a relative. We did not see the old lady ever again.

In the jungle, the people who die die from disease. In the Darien Gap, you can not forage or hunt, and so what you eat is what you bring with you, carried on your back for the entire 60 miles. We ate cookies with tuna but we drank water from the river, water we could not boil or disinfect or sanitize - water we would also bathe and defecate in. Sometimes, we would bend down, hands on the ground, and suck water from puddles in the mud. I myself got sick from a bacteria in my stomach from drinking the unfiltered water. I had this sickness when, on the second day, we had to cross a big mountain called "*La Llorona*," which was so hard to climb we needed to hold onto ropes pulled taut above the mud. In Venezuela, children know the legend of *La llorona*, a vengeful ghost, the spirit of a woman whose children were killed. She can be found near bodies of water where she drowns children who falter. In the jungle people who die die from sickness. One cannot falter.

In the jungle, the people who die die because they get raped or murdered. At night we slept in tents, and could hear people screaming, the sound of gunshots and children crying, and always the sound of rain. Every once in a while we would pass a tree with a blue ribbon tied around it - this was how we knew we were heading in the right direction. To get lost would be to invite death. In the three days we were in the jungle, I only saw one animal - a crocodile in the distance. But more dangerous animals surrounded us at every second.

There is no road through the jungle, not even a primitive one. Many people bypass it altogether. For those that would go through, like my mother and brother and myself, they must go through on foot. They must go through carefully. They must go through with courage and strength. They must go through together, or not at all.

KATHERINE MARTINEZ

(VENEZUELA)

THE NIGHT WE LEFT Punto Ardita the tide was strong and everyone was scared. We tied our life jackets tight around our chests.

To get from Colombia to Panama, many Venezuelans take the long road through the Darien Gap. Those that wish for a different route disembark here and voyage over the ocean with nothing but a sailor's hope for a safe journey over the rough seas.

On our very first night out of harbor our engine failed and we had to change boats, a task made all the more difficult because of the fact that we couldn't safely return to port. We had spent many hours drifting over the open water when the sky became pitch black and the first of the passengers started to vomit. Suddenly, there were three boats around us on the ocean, there to pick up and transport the people on our ship. I overheard one of the sailors talking angrily to another. He was upset because his boat was supposed to be full of 45 Chinese migrants, all of whom were missing.

We made it back to shore at midnight. For that entire day, we didn't eat anything. We took off our clothes and rinsed them to cleanse them of the salty water.

The next day we had to run to get on the boat to continue our journey, but once on board, we did not go in the direction we wanted. Instead, we went back to look for the missing Chinese, who we were told had reached a lonely and mountainous island, and were waiting there to be rescued. I don't know how many hours of sailing it was, only that there were a lot of waves and we were going too fast for all of them.

That night they left us in the bay, throwing all our clothes and belongings at us. We took our things and laid them in the sun.

A boat came from afar and we cried for help but they turned back because they saw that there were too many of us.

At night, the Chinese came down from the mountains and made a bonfire and prepared several crabs and we ate our bread with tuna. That night we wrapped ourselves in garbage bags and watched the bonfire and listened to the waves and prayed that it wouldn't rain and decided to put down stones on the sand and settle in for the night because the tide was going to rise and the river around us would also rise and perhaps the people would rise and we would be beset by danger from within and without.

We tied our life jackets tightly around our chests and prayed to be rescued.

JULIAN AGUILAR

(ECUADOR)

I T WAS OUR THIRD time trying to cross the border, and my father and I were becoming experts at each separate leg of the long journey.

The day we left home began in Ecuador with a short, three hour trip from Cuenca to Guayaquil. We were at the airport and my father asked if I wanted to eat but because of my nerves I couldn't. I was nauseous.

When we had to go through customs, we were very nervous. They took us into an interview room with about six other families - all of them headed to San Salvador. Half of those families were sent back, unable to pass because they were missing important information or had false documents.

We also had false documents, including one that said we were vaccinated against the yellow fever.

"*Si ustedes me dan mas dinero yo les puedo dar el documento para que no esperen y salgan ya de viaje*," the coyote had said to us, promising these papers would get us through. We accepted the deal only because we didn't have enough time to get our own. My stomach was in knots.

When we arrived in Bogota, Colombia we felt happy to have been able to leave our country but saddened by the sudden reality of being away from our family. We had to sleep on the floor without blankets, using our bags as pillows. I tried to fall asleep but the smell of sweat kept me awake. The stench was unbearable.

We left at eleven at night to get to Costa Rica, finally arriving three hours later. At six we arrived in El Salvador.

It felt like a lifetime as I sat there in the heat, but after an hour a car grabbed us from the airport. From there, they brought us to a gas station, where they told us to eat because we wouldn't have any more stops. We barely ate because our budget was very low.

Soon, we arrived at the border between El Salvador and Guatemala, and they took us to a field where we were forced to stay with the cows and horses to hide from the police. The stench of manure filled the air and their droppings stuck to our shoes as we tried to find a clean place to rest.

That night, we stayed at a house that belonged to some people who were carrying firearms and knives. We didn't eat. Finally, we arrived at the Mexican border where they put us in a house with a tin roof that made everything very hot and we waited there for a few hours before walking the rest of the way. There were mountains of garbage along the road, and next to them a river full of tires tied together with sticks and that's how we came to Tapachula, Mexico on a rubber river smelling of refuse.

For three days and three nights we lived in different hotels. Eventually, we boarded a bus bound for Oaxaca. In Oaxaca we were able to buy forged papers so we could travel the rest of the way by plane and so, from Oaxaca we made it to Monterrey and from Monterrey to Tijuana. At this point, we were with a woman who had a daughter who was about six months old. Those days we went out to eat. One of those days we ate hamburgers made from some kind of crocodile and the next day we ate chocolate and banana shakes and tacos.

Many planes and cars and buses carried us on our journey, but from Tijuana we walked through the desert, finally making it into America on foot. We planted our feet in free soil. It was our third attempt, and the third time was the charm.

Slowly, but inevitably, we made it to the United States.

BRENDA HERNANDEZ

(HONDURAS)

W E WERE SOMEWHERE IN Mexico on the edge of the desert when the police detected our van. It was around three in the morning, but we were all of us up, squeezed together, shaking. I could hear the shouts through the insulated walls of the vehicle, and was very scared - so scared I began praying to God that nothing would happen.

The driver of the van was less composed, and began driving so fast he lost control. We smashed headfirst into some cacti.

"You're in danger!" the police shouted, their cars some hundred or so feet from ours, and as if to prove themselves right they began shooting. We knew we had to quickly leave before we wound up dead.

"Run," the coyotes shouted at me and my aunt. "Run!"

When we ran, we scattered, each heading in a different direction. I ran so far and so fast I outran even my thoughts. It could only have been seconds, but it felt like hours had passed when I suddenly realized I was alone.

I was running even faster now, through some thorny bushes, when I found a woman crying. She had been in my van with her three-year-old daughter. I noticed she was alone and in tears. I told her not to worry, that we would find her daughter. But most urgently I told her "You have to keep running!"

We heard gunshots nearby. Through the darkness I could see a man waving a gun. My friend fell, terrified.

"Keep going," she screamed! "Fight for what you want! Don't die here."

"I won't leave you alone," I cried, and lifted her up to her feet.

We ran until we were exhausted; ran until our feet were numb and our lungs were on fire, and our minds crossed over, delirious with fatigue and thirst and fear. We eventually collapsed in a bush.

At dawn the next day, we were found by our guide. He said they were looking for us everywhere. He brought us back to the van. My aunt was there. Others we hoped to find weren't.

It didn't matter. We were still so far from our goal.

We had to keep running.

ALY TREJO

(HONDURAS)

T HE SHOTS FROM THE black van behind us were the last things we heard before my mother and I made the decision to jump from the moving car and take our chances in the mountains. We didn't know whether or not we could survive the journey through the thorns and bramble, but we knew we would never survive an encounter with the armed soldiers behind us. In Mexico, it's inadvisable to get caught by the police, but it is deadly to be captured by *Los Zetas*— a Mexican drug cartel known as the most dangerous criminal syndicate in all of North and South America.

Although primarily invested in drugs, *Los Zetas* have branched into sex trafficking, protection rackets, and the occasional indiscriminate rape and beheading. Every one of us knew the story of the 72 migrants who were found in a mass grave in Tamaulipas— the Mexican state where *Los Zetas* have the most control. That this failed state lied between us and Texas meant we had to pay off the Cartel for safe passage or else suffer a similar fate. For this, we trusted the coyote we had given money to on our way from Honduras.

Instead of making the proper pay-offs, however, our coyote decided to keep the money for himself. Looking back, it might have been obvious. The car we traveled in was itself stolen. I remember when we first got in after leaving the safehouse the driver and the navigator had to jump the car with power cables to even get it to start. They had walkie-talkies, and would speak to other vans.

"There are no cops at the next post," I heard during one of their conversations. It seemed too easy, and I felt fear and anguish over what could go wrong. Soon, it became clear that the coyote did not pay *Los Zetas* and, having not paid, the *Zetas* would chase, kidnap, and kill us.

It was at this moment that my mother and I jumped from the car while it was still moving. We lifted our heads just in time to see *Los Zetas* rush past us, their black car like Death on the night wind.

We had to crawl along the edge of the wall where it was full of thorns until we reached a small cave entrance. The only thing I wanted at that moment was to be with my family, but I wondered what would happen if we were caught. I don't really know where I got the strength to encourage my mother to continue but, for fear of what would happen if we stopped, we moved on.

We walked through human bones— standing graves where people had died, or were killed. Sometimes, we had to hide in hills or caves because of helicopters that would pass above us. We knew that even if they couldn't see us with their eyes, the helicopters of *Los Zetas* could target our body heat on their sensors, and could find the signals from our electric devices in their scans. We had to camouflage ourselves on the ground, pressing our bodies into the dirt, and move only at dawn when our heat could not be distinguished from the desert air. We walked through paths that had been made by others, and past the dying and the dead. We had no water or food and were always afraid.

I remember one day we found a tunnel, black as the truck against a starless night. We did not know where it went— whether to America or back to the *Zetas*. Or perhaps to nowhere.

We took one tentative step in. Then another.

JOSE MATZAR

(GUATEMALA)

"Hago realidad los sueños."

The smuggling of human beings is a financially lucra-
tive business, but it was for dreams, not dollars, that my
coyote insisted he got up in the morning.

In truth, the fees he charged were modest enough. To
guarantee the successful passage of human cargo, coyotes
charge a variable rate depending on their expertise and
method of travel. The prices start at around $3000 for the
most basic package, up to $6000 for a trip that could be
said to be a little more premium, all the way up to $15,000
for the VIP experience.

My family could not afford the VIP experience.
Nevertheless, because my sister and I were children, our
coyote stayed with us around the clock, mostly in the
cabin of the trailer where we traveled in secret. We were
among the lucky ones. Many immigrants don't have the
resources to hire a guide at all, and so walk across Mexico

on foot. Sometimes we would stop at gas stations along the way to go to the bathroom. Sometimes we would eat.

In Mexico, my coyote said, good people pay him to protect their loved ones. But only God can protect the coyote.

"I see hundreds of families, but rarely my own," he told me. "The last time was after I had been in prison for nine months. After all that time my family finally had enough money to bail me out. Since then they have doubled their prayers."

The coyote network is organizational, structured with multiple levels of workers. In the towns and villages across South America there are the interior coyotes, the recruiters who develop social capital and trust. Then there are the higher level coyotes that take the migrants to hotels near the border. Then, finally, a last coyote that takes you into America. At all times and at each step, these coyotes are supported by a vast network of surveillance, specially trained coyotes skilled as lookouts. When my sister and I switched between different workers in the organization, we would be identified by a red bracelet. This meant we had paid.

Still, the system of human smuggling is not perfect.

It was in Reynosa that we were surrounded by the Mexican National Guard, cornered by patrols who threatened to send us all back to Guatemala. The police approached the car and asked my sister and me and the other people in the car what we were going to do, but no one who was there wanted to answer the officers' questions. They asked the coyote why he was leading several people but he denied any wrongdoing. Finally, the police offered a bargain: the coyote could pay a bribe and go free, or keep his money and go to jail. They demanded nothing more and nothing less than 45,000 Mexican Pesos, an exorbitant amount of money equivalent to almost $3000.

Eventually, my coyote coughed up the ransom. Within the hour, we were saying goodbye.

"Take care," I said. "Think about God."

"*Piensa en tu sueño,*" he said. "*Ahora hazlo realidad.*"

There were many things I wanted to say. But it was already too late. He was gone, off to give another family what he could not give himself.

I waved goodbye as we crossed the border into America.

MISHELL CHAMBA BENITEZ

(ECUADOR)

THE DAY WE CROSSED the Rio Grande and made our final escape into America, I woke up afraid, startled by loud knocking at my door in the very early hours of the morning.

"Let's go! Let's go," they shouted. "We are waiting for you outside in the van! Come or you'll be left behind."

It was pitch black and I was half asleep, but somehow I was able to find my shoes and help my sister find hers. I was scared, not knowing what was going to happen or where we were heading, but I piled into the van along with the coyotes. Soon, we arrived at a small clearing among the trees and animals. It was not quite sunrise, and the light of the moon offered no warmth or illumination. It was cold and we were shivering.

I was tired and hungry - we had no food or water - and as we walked through the forest I wondered how much longer we would have to go and how we would cross the river when we got there. But as the eldest sister I decided to keep quiet, wanting to maintain my composure to calm my frightened siblings.

Finally, still in total darkness, we arrived at the banks of the Rio Grande. Two men already there showed us our ship, an orange and yellow inflatable raft, a toy meant for children and the calm, clear, shallow waters of their backyard pools. It was maybe seven feet long and 3 feet wide. Empty of passengers, it looked like it was already ready to deflate.

The men gave us a life jacket and explained how to get into the inflatable boat, how to paddle, and what we would have to do after reaching the other shore. Most importantly, they told us, we had to remain silent. I continued to be scared, afraid something would happen to us in the middle of the river. My family is all I have, and I didn't want anything bad to happen to them. There were seven of us altogether, and no way to all fit side by side. I grabbed my little brother and sat him on my legs, while my mother held tight to my other two siblings.

We had made it to the middle of the river when the coyote heard a noise he thought might be the immigration police. He stopped the boat. Bobbing in the middle of the river, thinking at any moment I could go under, I was suddenly overwhelmed by terror and despair, desperate with the urge to burst into tears. I held it together for the sake of my siblings.

After about twenty minutes we reached the other side. My legs felt so weak and fragile and I felt like I couldn't walk without fainting. My mother, twice as numb, stood up and encouraged us to continue.

There was no time for relief, or to celebrate setting foot on American soil as - suddenly - we were told we had to run to get to our next destination, a car the coyotes had previously arranged. If we walked or went too slowly, we could still be found by immigration. My sister started crying, loudly howling that she had lost her shoe. She yelled and yelled, screaming that she couldn't go on.

My sister's cries penetrated through the darkness. I was nervous and still scared, not knowing how to process everything that had happened since I woke up. I thought about all the powerful emotions I was going through, and I thought about crossing the deep waters of the Rio Grande, and I thought about how if one wants to make it successfully to America, it is important not to drown in either.

KEVIN DUCHITANGA

(ECUADOR)

T HE BORDER WALL THAT divides Mexico and Arizona is tall and long and, for those of us who come on foot, an intimidating end to a journey of thousands of miles. On the trek from Mexico City to Naco to a series of cabins near the border, we had been told that the Wall would test our spirit, that we would have to climb and jump and scramble over the fence to make it to America. Even for the athletic and strong, the Wall presented additional challenges, our guide explained, as there are hidden wires and small plates around and throughout. If any of us touched these in the wrong places, Border Patrol would immediately be alerted to our presence and come to snatch us.

The Wall is strong, but its greatest strength is that the Wall has eyes and ears.

Many of the migrants we met along our journey spoke of the Wall, but conversation became much more focused the closer we got to Arizona. It was in a small house just outside of Naco, Mexico - south of the American border - where we began to learn exactly what we were facing.

In that house, there were already many dozens of people who were also emigrating, and we had to stay there for a week as we waited for a coyote to arrive. The people who were there told us they had been there for five months already, and that we should expect a long wait - a purgatory close to Heaven but still so far away. Some people told us to buy gloves, bandages, and knee pads to help us cross the border, because the road was very dangerous and we would have to crawl most of it.

We assumed that we would be there for many weeks, but in a silence of a second, we heard them say "the Duchitanga family." We were shocked and not prepared, and only had a twenty minute warning to get ready. They gave us military armor to camouflage, and backpacks with food and survival gear, and off we went to the mountains.

The backpacks were heavy and the mountain was steep, so by the time we got to the top it was already evening. There, we saw a small, pink house which was to be our rest for the night. The guide told us we were not allowed to leave. We were hungry and thirsty and, again, met people that had been in this house for months.

The next morning they began to take people in groups of four to the border. We thought we would be there for many days, but were again shocked when the guide called our name. Outside of our backpacks, we were told to bring only water.

The path was very difficult and the heavy backpack wore me down. After long hours I felt exhausted. I had to carry a large, heavy backpack of objects - survival supplies such as water, food, and first aid kits. After long hours I already felt tired and exhausted, but luckily I found a young man named Marcel who helped me by carrying my backpack the rest of the way.

For the first leg of the journey we would walk normally along a path of small rocks and tree spikes, but soon the guide said we had to continue crawling. And then we understood why the knee pads, bandages, and gloves were necessary. For a long time we crawled, and the bandages and the knee pads were not of much use - at one point mine broke, and I had to crawl on my elbows. My feet and joints hurt and bled, and I saw that my mom and cousin were also in pain.

Suddenly, our guide told us to run, and immediately we were up and at full-speed, desperate to evade the police. While running I fell twice, but each time I didn't care about the pain, only that I had to get up and continue going as fast as I could. Soon, we could run no further and stopped at a little tree that provided some shade. This was lucky because we heard over the walkie-talkie that the police had converged on our last known location, and that by staying still they might not discover us. We stayed there for two long hours and in those two hours we had no water. Our bodies began to be eaten by ants.

Under the tree I became sleepy. While I was crawling I was nervous and afraid because I was worried that maybe immigration would find us and report us or that something would happen to my family in the desert and that we would have to abandon them and possibly let them die. But suddenly I heard a voice and it was the guide's and he began to explain that everything would turn out well. We knew the journey was not going to be easy and that bad things could happen, but we also knew we were going to suffer whatever it was in pursuit of a better future. Part of me wanted to repent, to be forgiven for coming, to turn back and return to my home.

But then another part of me spoke through the fatigue. "I'm almost there," I said to myself. "Everything I've done so far cannot be in vain."

Again the radio came alive and again, it told us ro run. We thought only about our feet, and about the Wall, and about what would happen when they met.

Finally, we could see it on the horizon.

We saw The Wall. We saw The Wall had large doors.

We saw that the doors of The Wall were wide open.

MARIELVIS TABLANTE
(VENEZUELA)

T HE FIRST THING IMMIGRATION and Customs ask for when they catch you crossing the border is your identification papers - licenses, passports, anything that could put a legal name to your case. The second thing they ask for is your shoelaces. The third thing ICE ask you for is everything else. What they can't ask for they will take. And what they can take - your name, your clothes, your dignity - they can never give back.

I breathed hard and fast, afraid. We were heading towards *las hieleras*.

I prayed. I prayed the whole way.

***

Sometimes called the icebox, or the freezer, or just the coolers, these cramped, frigid holding cells are common experiences for migrants on the very last leg of their long journeys, particularly for women and children.

What nobody can prepare you for is that the names don't do the experience justice: The cells are freezing, especially for those of us still wet from crossing the river. In this place there are walls, but also walls made of plastic, thin film with large tubes that expel a cold that penetrates your bones. When we first arrived officers took our fingerprints and weighed us. They tested us for COVID. My mother held my hand during this whole process.

"I'm scared," I told her, digging my nails into the palm of her hand.

"Don't be scared," she said. But her voice trembled in the cold.

More and more people arrived. Soon, they separated the women from the men, and the children from the adults. I was all alone and stripped, asked to remove every piece of clothing I had and told to enter a shower. My head hurt and so in the shower I didn't wash my hair but the officer saw this and forced me to.

When I got out, the pain in my head intensified to the point that I started to cry. My crying was getting worse and so they took me to the doctor. I was shaking from the cold, my hair still wet, and had a terrible headache.

They gave me medicine. They gave me an apple. They gave me a blanket like tin foil to wrap around my body when I slept on the floor. That night I spent with my mother but not with my brother. We didn't know where or how he was. Every hour the officers would knock on the doors. The echo was horrible and we could hardly sleep. The babies especially cried. At dawn they gave us a burrito and some juice.

Already separated from my brother, the next night they further isolated me by separating me from my mother as well. I went to a room with only teenage girls like myself.

"How many days have you been here," I asked them.

"Two days," one said.

"I heard that some people are forced to spend weeks," another one chimed in.

We spent two days like this. Or maybe one. Or maybe it was forever and I'm still there. Time had no meaning in the icebox. When you fell asleep, they would wake you up to take everything out of the room and clean. When you came back, there might be different people there. Or none at all. Or maybe you were moved, or the whole world was. I thought maybe they would send me back. Or that I would never leave. We never knew if it was day or night.

And, sometimes, when you are in the dominion of ICE, it would get so cold in *las hieleras* that you couldn't tell if the freeze was coming from outside your body, or if it had finally turned to winter in your heart.

JEYSI GARCIA

(GUATEMALA)

IN 1992 MY FATHER left Guatemala and traveled to the United States, but was caught and turned away in Mexico. So the second time he tried, he knew he had to take an even harder road.

To avoid detection, this time my father traveled through the mountains. Alone, and not knowing the way, he quickly became lost, wandering throughout the peaks for three months before crossing to the other side.

On this journey, he had to endure rain and cold, heat and hunger, and thirst most of all. During this time, my father fed on birds and rabbits that he managed to hunt and catch with simple traps. He made these traps with stones, stakes and rope.

To catch the birds he would use worms for bait. To catch the rabbits he would make holes in the ground and cover them with leaves so that the rabbits would fall in.

For 90 days he walked. And for 90 nights. My father believed that this journey would be the end of him, and that he would starve to death, or die from thirst. He thought all of his efforts would be in vain.

I asked him, once, why he kept going.

He said that although my older sister and I were not yet born, he carried us in his heart. My father carried us as a lucky charm that would help him cross safely - that we were my father's light to continue moving forward, the light that illuminated the dark and difficult path he had to cross. When my father was tired, the two of us were the ones who gave him the energy to continue walking. My father's pockets were full of love that had not yet arrived - our love for him and of his love towards us.

After three months of suffering, he crossed into America.

America, where, because my father hunted rabbits and birds, we could buy food.

Where, because my father crossed borders, I could grow up a citizen.

Where, because my father was lost in the mountains, I could find my home.

ALLINSON DIAZ

(HONDURAS)

I<small>T WAS A COUPLE</small> months out of Honduras - first by plane to El Salvador, then by car to Guatemala, and finally by foot and flotilla to the United States - when I took command over a group of migrants, including my mother and brother. For months we had journeyed, danger at our backs, and now we had walked straight into it: we were barely across the Texas border when we were ambushed by American immigration officers, guns in the air, demanding our obedience.

My mother pushed me forward. She knew what I knew: out of the twenty of us who had hired the coyote, ridden together in buses, and finally swam to freedom, I was the only one who knew any English.

I had learned some in first grade.

"Hands up," the officer ordered. "Take your shoes off." This I knew. I knew hands. I knew shoes. I knew up and off. By the time he said what I thought was "Empty your pockets!" however, my translation had crossed into complete fabrication. It didn't matter. I did what I thought was right, and spoke to the others in Spanish so that they might do the same. As the only English speaking person of the group, I became the translator - a task that I enjoyed, as it appeared to calm the anxiety of the immigrant strangers I was now stuck with. Translating became a game I could win. I smiled and laughed. They smiled and laughed.

Proud, I grabbed my mother's hand so that we could walk to the car together. It was then that I noticed her eyes screaming for help, her lips shivering in panic, afraid to make even a single small noise. I didn't know how to protect her, but felt the incredible, sudden urge to stay quiet. We walked to the immigration officers, making sure to go slowly, and deliberately, and to always walk one foot in front of the other, directly straight ahead.

We were in jail for three days before being released.

***

For many years after, as we began to settle in this new country, my duties began to grow and become more difficult. My mother had to work to help my father as we struggled with financial hardship, leaving me to take on the responsibilities of the house. With no complaints, I took care of my brothers, performed the household chores, and aided my mom with her new jobs: babysitting and cleaning. This became not just my character, but my destiny, as I found comfort in the happiness of others, consumed by the exhilaration I felt from a smile or a laugh. As my roles increased, so too did my burden, no longer eight but still responsible for the lives of so many.

One day, deep into my junior year of high school, I was helping a friend with her assignment for school. Her job was to interview adults for health class. Deeply underwater with my own work, I nevertheless took on hers as well, and spoke to the subjects on her behalf.

"What do you think is the secret to a successful marriage?"

"What's one thing people don't know about having kids?"

"What piece of advice would you give to young kids in a relationship?"

My own experience with relationships was minimal, and I didn't always understand their answers. It didn't matter. I translated what I thought was right.

My entire life I had been full of joy from this kind of sacrifice, but that evening I found myself overwhelmed with the need to give up. Looking in the mirror, I saw my mother's eyes, and felt as though I was screaming for help, but covering my own mouth to protect others.

My mind began to race. I didn't know how to protect myself, but felt the incredible, sudden urge to stay quiet.

I thought back to the desert, to the long journey that had led there, to the many journeys since that put me in this room - a bizarre series of accidents, any one of which could have changed everything. It's such a long road as an immigrant. I make a resolution:

I will go slowly. And deliberately. And each day I will make sure to always walk one foot in front of the other, directly straight ahead.

PART THREE

BETWEEN TWO WORLDS

I FELT TORN AND CONFUSED, NOT KNOWING WHO I REALLY WAS OR WHERE I REALLY BELONGED.

EMILIA SANTOS

(PORTUGAL)

THE DAY I DIED started like any other normal day. My friends and I were planning to go to a water park in the Pocono Mountains to eat unhealthy food and watch movies and stay up late. Instead, I began to suffer from a terrible headache, drifting in and out of what I felt like was the present moment, as the things that tethered me to the here and now washed away. I called my mother, crying. She told me to stay still and that she would take me to the hospital.

I don't remember anything after that.

***

The day the old Portugal died was officially April 25, 1974, in a bloodless and swift military coup eventually known as the Carnation Revolution. This followed decades of authoritarian rule, and more recently, years of general disarray as the body politic moved towards the inevitable moment it would attack itself. In this time, citizens were under great fear of breaking any of a number of rules, both known and unknown. Portugal's first free election was held a year later.

Into this turbulence, a few months after the election, my mother was born.

Before her birth, my grandparents were terrified that the silent war in Portugal would continue, but in the months and years after the country became more and more open - books, poems, songs, or even newspapers were no longer limited or cut off. Lessons in class were not removed through threat of violence, and American movies played in local cinemas. Anyone could do what they pleased, even hug their loved ones in public.

My mother really liked the hugging, as from the start, she was the kind of person who would stop everything to help someone she loved. No doubt for this reason, she was chosen among her siblings to join my grandfather as the only two members of the family to immigrate to America when an economic crisis of gigantic proportions necessitated that a few of them must leave for another country. My aunt stayed in Portugal to complete her education. My uncle took over the family farm. But my mother - still a child herself - chose to drop everything and travel across the ocean in search of a way to help.

Over time, my mother and grandfather were supposed to get a house, work, get money, and attempt to become citizens in the United States but when they got here, it was difficult for them to find a home to live in. They had to work day and night to bring their family over. Eventually, even that was not enough time and so my mother had to drop out of East Side High School as a senior to have even more time for labor. To this day, she's never graduated high school.

***

The Carnation Revolution got its name from a restaurant worker who offered flowers to the soldiers as the people took to the streets in celebration. Others followed suit and began placing flowers in the gun barrels and muzzles of all the soldiers. Almost no shots were fired.

***

Supposedly, I was still awake on the way to the hospital, yet I was not aware or conscious of my on-going personhood. I still had a heartbeat, and paramedics could still measure my blood pressure, but I could neither move nor answer questions.

Once at the hospital, I was moved quickly to another room to begin surgery on my brain. In the operating room, one of the nurses realized that the pupil in my right eye was dilating quickly and they thought that it might be connected to blood running through my brain.

This issue is called a brain Arteriovenous Malformation, or AVM. An AVM is when a blood vessel irregularly connects to arteries and veins in the brain. This can lie dormant for years or even decades, until the pressure is so great it explodes. To fix this problem, they not only had to remove the blood vessel but the area of the brain surrounding it that was damaged due to the explosion.

When the doctors were done with the surgeries, I was left to sleep for as long as it took for my body to awaken, but I was in a coma for many weeks. Nobody knew how I would be if and when I woke up. They didn't know if I would be able to speak, or read, or move, or see, or think. They didn't know if the person who woke up would be able to feel - if the person who woke up would even, in any real sense, be me at all.

When I did finally wake up after almost a month I woke up disoriented and terrified.

I tried to get myself off the machines that were connected to what felt like every part of me, but I could not move anything on the right side of my body. The more I moved my head, the more I realized I couldn't see major areas of what used to be my field of vision. I tried to yell - to scream - but nothing came out of my mouth.

My dad held me down, saying words I heard but could not understand, words I learned later were calls for help, begging for a doctor to come.

And somewhere it registered that the last thing I remembered was that it was autumn, and now the window in my room clearly showed a winter sky.

***

During the build-up to the Portuguese Revolution, my father's parents chose to leave their home country and live in Germany. My father was born there soon after, and, when my grandparents decided it might be safer to stay in case violence returned to Portugal, grew up there as well. They learned German quickly and began to get comfortable in their new surroundings.

In my father's childhood, he enjoyed many things like learning about history or science, playing soccer, hanging out with friends, and walking around his city. Since my grandparents owned many businesses, they were rarely home and, because of this, my father learned self-reliance and independence from an early age.

Soon, an economic crisis of gigantic proportions necessitated that the family move once again, this time to the United States. My father only had a month to get comfortable in America before school started, and so found it very difficult to make friends because, lacking any understanding of English, the people around him would communicate only in words he did not understand. No doubt as a result, he never really focused on academics at East Side High School, where he was a student.

He managed to do well into his senior year, when a counselor began to ask questions about what colleges he wanted to go to. It was then that he realized as an immigrant he had no options, except perhaps the military. Lacking both any motivation and help, he chose to leave school early and work with my grandparents at various businesses. Hard, physical work became the new normal. To this day, he's never graduated high school.

***

In Portugal, the period after the first democratic election in 1975 was known as the *Processo Revolucionário em Curso* or the "Ongoing Revolutionary Process." I like that: "The Ongoing Revolutionary Process." Many say this process never ended.

***

I stayed at the hospital for almost two months when COVID-19 blanketed America. Here, my daily schedule was constant and unchanging: I would wake up in silence and go through what felt like millions of different therapies without a word. I would force myself to power through the pain to move my leg or arm just one centimeter, but would fail often. Nurses would have to help me eat and clean.

During this time, I began to feel like I lost myself, even as everyone around me tried to make me smile. I was numb. I began to forget who I truly was and might have completely, were it not for the fact that by the end of my stay at the hospital I started to write again. I wrote the words I couldn't say and I spoke about the words that I forgot how to spell. Soon, I was able to walk from the chair to the bed. I kept urging myself to practice over and over until I could get back to my normal life, even as I knew I never would.

When they sent me home, they gave my parents a walking-stick and a wheelchair and urged me to use it and to not harm my body. I did not listen. When I got home, I left these tools of disability in the other room and began to try to walk on my own. I would fall every single day but I did not care. I did not want to be seen as crippled, and never wanted to be considered "strong" just because I had to go through a traumatic event. My biggest motivation was to avoid ever being stared at for being weak.

By April, I was told to join online classes even though I was not supposed to go back to school until June. I was still dealing with issues in instructions, speech, understanding, and overall memory. This destroyed me. I used to be one of the smartest kids in my grade, and now I felt stupid. Over the summer, I kept to myself in my room, studying and re-learning concepts of grammar and math I knew I had learned years before.

In the years since I woke up in the hospital bed, much has improved while much has stayed the same.

The process is still ongoing.

***

In Newark, everyone ends up knowing everyone else although it took longer for my parents to meet than one would think given that they went to the same high school and attended the same Portuguese cultural events. By their late twenties, my father was living with a baby - my brother Alex - and my mother was still living with my grandparents, mostly so she could help my grandmother. It was very difficult for them to find a job because of their schedules - schedules which made it even more difficult to have a personal life.

They met at one of the lowest points in each of their lives.

After a year of dating they got married and had me. They changed their schedules to be able to take care of my brother and I, and still work to give their children a better life than they had. My mother was able to become a citizen, and my father was able to learn the language.

They have struggled so hard as immigrants. They have struggled so hard as parents.

***

These are such delicate things. The carnation goes into the muzzle and the clot goes into the vessel and the people clog the city streets like arteries, bumping into each other as they find their destinies. Do you see how close it all is to exploding?

***

Currently I am still partly blind, still considered disabled, still missing words in English, Portuguese, and Spanish. Many days I still feel lost - a stranger in the world of normal people. My parents were there and now they are here. I was here, and now I'm there, an immigrant from a world we are not supposed to return from. My family stops everything to help me. They are my light in the ever-growing darkness. This year I will graduate high school with the highest honors.

That day, like every day now, I will be born again, thrust into a world that is mine alone.

BEAU AMBROISE

(MALAYSIA)

A s we made our way through the busy streets of my mother's native country of Malaysia, the air was thick with the aroma of spices.

"Try the *laksa*, Beau. It's one of my favorites. The way they make it in America doesn't come close to how they do it here," my mother said excitedly as we sat down at a street-side eatery.

I looked into the steaming hot bowl with skepticism. The noodles and the soup glowed a vibrant red, further conveying their heat.

"It's spicy, right?" I asked my mother, recalling my past experiences with Malaysian heat. I was worried.

"Just try it. It'll be the best thing ever," she responded.

The spiciness was too much for my young, American palate, and the flavors were strong and potent. Despite the blending of Chinese and Malaysian cuisine, everything on the table seemed foreign. Instead of enjoying the local cuisine, the aisles of American supermarkets became my haven, where I sought comfort in the familiar foods.

My family's dinners became a dance of give and take. They enjoyed the authentic taste of Malaysian food, but I clung to my staples from America - a culinary apartheid that meant I couldn't participate in their meals or memories.

It took a long time for me after I left Malaysia to understand the cultural tug-of-war I was involved in.

"You know, your grandparents would be proud to see you embrace their culture," my mother said, preparing a Malaysian dish.

She often added a touch of Malaysian spice to my bland American meals - even if the tastes did not match perfectly, every meal served as a bridge that opened my eyes to a world outside America. As my palette grew, so did my tolerance for spicy foods.

One day, my mother made me a dish similar to the laksa I couldn't consume as a kid. It had the same runny eggs and shrimp, and the smell of the noodles burnt my nostrils. As I savored the complex tastes of the dish which previously overwhelmed me, I realized how much my love for Malaysian food had grown.

My mother had done it: she had shared with me her heritage, an entire world of Malaysia that screamed to be discovered and appreciated. And she did it slowly - one dish at a time.

JOSUE SOARES

(BRAZIL)

F OR MANY YEARS I lived as a stranger in America, hidden
first from the people in my city who knew nothing of
my culture or heritage, and then from my own family,
who knew nothing of the real me.

It was when I decided to come out as gay that at least
I could stop being a stranger to myself.

The period of my own acceptance was difficult,
especially because I lived in an extremely homophobic
home, with a whole family of Brazilian evangelicals.
Without knowing they were talking about their own son
and grandson, many times I had heard them say that
all homosexuals go to Hell. This is doubly concentrated
generational hate, forged in the fires of both religion and
culture. To this day, Brazil struggles with wide-spread
LGBTQ acceptance - for instance, although same-sex
marriage and anti-discriminatory statutes are enshrined

in federal law, Brazil is ranked number one in the world in murders of trans people.

I hid my true identity from my entire family and started to create a personality that wasn't mine. It was around this time that I developed bulimia. The pressure of being someone other than who I was made me feel trapped in my own body, and I began to transfer that feeling into a belief that I wasn't good enough. I wanted to be the perfect child and that became wanting the perfect body. I would go to school and throw up everything I ate to make myself feel better. Soon, I became incredibly depressed, and could no longer imagine myself having any kind of future. I didn't see hope in the situation or hope in myself.

The first person I told I was gay was my mother. It was difficult to come out, and I could sense it was a blow to her.

Not long after, a week before my birthday, my mother got into an argument with my grandmother. During this fight my mother got angry and flustered and, in an attempt to hurt my grandmother, said the most spiteful and hateful thing she could think of: that I was gay and that she loved me anyway.

She loved me anyway, she said.

My evangelical grandmother, full of prejudice, said that she would pray to break the "curse" gayness had in me. I asked her if she thought that I would go to Hell for loving another man. She said yes.

"Then I'll go down to Hell, pole dancing the whole way down!" I said.

She told me I was no longer welcome in her home, which was also my home, where I lived with my mother and grandmother. Again, I felt nothing but pain, not knowing what to do or where to go.

Suddenly, my mother put her hand on my shoulder.

"Keep calm," she said. "We will find a place to live together."

When I was a boy, I was proud to say that I was Brazilian. We had a lot of joys in life, like songs and samba. I remember when I lived in Brazil and I went to my great-grandfather's house. He lived on a farm where they had a lot of trees, and I would hide in the branches, at total liberty to climb and swing and play.

After that day at my grandmother's, my mother and I moved out. Today, I climb and swing and play through the urban jungle, free to be me, in a place where I no longer have to hide from the world or myself.

ANGELLA CHARLES

(HAITI)

W HEN I WAS IN Haiti my friends used to do many fun activities outside at night. They would play "*Lago*," where someone has to run after a group of people, or "*Marelle*." But my parents were not fans of silly games.

"*Manman mka al jwe avek yo tou*," I would beg.

But my mother wouldn't let me join them, no matter how often I asked. Sometimes, I would go outside against my parents' will. In those times, there was laughter, many uncontrollable noises, lots of messy things. That's how happy we were.

When I came to America, I was really excited about the idea of being safer, surrounded by more people. I imagined myself with lots of friends, always playing in a park with them, and it gave me butterflies. But it was the complete opposite. For the first few weeks, when I ventured outside it was "*li te an silans tankou on simityè*."

I wanted to go outside, but I couldn't. I wanted to play, but I couldn't. Unlike in Haiti, there was no outside. And, worse, even when there were kids my age, I couldn't play with them because of our language differences.

"*Manman, pouki timoun yo pa soti deyo?*" I asked my mother, wondering why the children didn't go outside to play.

"*Se konsa peyi aletranje ye pitit.*" she answered. "That's how foreign countries are my child."

When I was a little kid, I had classes in English, but learned just the basics.

"Good morning, class."

"Good morning, teacher."

"How are you doing?"

"I'm doing good, thanks, and you?"

When I started to go to school it was really difficult to understand what my classmates were saying. I wanted to feel like I belonged. In Haiti, I was always in activities or programs, but here I couldn't join because I was afraid to pronounce something wrong and get laughed at. Sometimes I asked "*kijan yo di sa an angle?*" but I never repeated when they told me how to say the word in English.

Over time, I began to realize just how much I was missing. For lunch in my country we would go out, enjoy the outdoors, play and eat and share our food. But here, I just sat there in a corner, watching the others lining up. I wasn't smiling as much as I used to, and definitely talked less.

I was so desperate to fit in. I started to dress, speak, and even act like the American students did.

"Hey, wassup?"

"I'm good, how are you doing?"

"I'm doing great!"

My parents were so proud of me. But it wasn't the same with my other family members. It was rare for me to talk with them on the phone because I started to lose my native accent. For me to finally press the record button and send a voice memo to my friends back in Haiti took me an eternity. I had to repeat my message over and over again to manage an authentic accent. The more time passed, the less we talked.

I could hear them say with disappointment "*ou change ampil wi,*" laughing at how much I changed. I knew they were right. When I was with them, there was laughter, many uncontrollable noises, lots of messy things. Then, suddenly, everything was different. We hardly talk at all now.

Them and their silly games.

"*Se konsa peyi aletranje ye pitit,*" I say now about them. That's how foreign countries are, my child.

MARIA QUINTAO

(BRAZIL)

After my mom got arrested, my dad wanted absolutely nothing to do with her, not even to take me and my sisters to visit her in immigration lock-up. That responsibility fell on my senile great-grandmother: Vovo. The first time Vovo took my sisters and I to visit my mom, I was 9, Carol was 14 and Bella wasn't even a year old. I was nervous. There were numerous circular tables around us, with other families seeing their loved ones, each convict wearing an unusual blue-gray uniform with an off-white shirt underneath. At the time, only a month had passed since her arrest, yet it felt like years. We were all excited to see her, but something felt off.

It had only been a month, but it felt like she had already missed out on some of my scholastic achievements. Her shoulder length hair was now down to her chest. Even her scent began to change. The smell of coffee and cigarettes had once been synonymous with my mother but now she smelled vaguely of butterscotch and clean rags. Her face looked different as well. The woman who stood before me looked tired. The once menacing eyes that glared at me when angered were now puffy and red. A voice that trembled the entire house, even when just speaking normally, was now quiet and raspy.

These visits soon became less about her kids, and more "adult talk" instead. I soon dreaded coming to visit and slept through most conversations.

According to my mom, she was arrested for a minor misdemeanor - something like jaywalking. Unfortunately for my mom, even children know that criminal records are public, and after a quick Google search, we found out she was stealing mail from people. My mom was now a federal criminal.

***

My mom got deported not long after her arrest. She stayed at a cousin's house in São Paulo for the most part and visited my dad's side of the family in Minas Gerais for about a week. Her experience coming back after years of being away from her home country was very scary for her. Though the language never changed, the people and environment around her did. Compared to America it felt unsafe, she said. She often heard gunshots outside her home, and was worried for her safety and that of her cousins.

Barely a month had passed when she traveled to Cancun to start the process of crossing the border again. In this repeat process, she faced many problems, some similar to the first time she migrated, some brand new. At one point, the coyotes in charge of her safety sent her to the wrong men, and she was kidnapped alongside another Brazilian girl. My dad, grandma and Vovo had to help pay the $2,000 ransom to release her.

Soon, she was able to cross at El Paso. After going around a few other cities in Texas, she was able to get on a bus to Ohio. In Ohio she met up with a friend who then drove her to New Jersey.

In a lot of ways, it felt like she never left. At first, she was kinder and more attentive. I began to hope that she actually learned what she almost lost because of stupid decisions. However, her old habits slowly crept back. The mood in the house shifted once again and now everything was back to "normal."

***

One day my sister got a call from my dad. "Your mom got arrested again."

Thankfully, this time it wasn't because of a felony but because of a previous legal issue which was never resolved. She was in the middle of delivering for DoorDash when a passing police cruiser stopped her because of the hour. They found old warrants and arrested her on the spot, and she stayed in jail for eight months before getting released under house arrest with an ankle monitor. This time her return wasn't as dramatic, and I didnt cry either. She pretended to have changed but soon slipped back into her old behavior. Eventually, her probation officer told her she had until the 15th of September to leave the country. It came as a surprise to all of us.

My mom is known for lousy, half-assed apologies. It's something I had grown accustomed to. Imagine my surprise, then, when my mom was in the middle of driving me to school and decided to have a heart-to-heart. She apologized for everything that happened in the past few years, and for any recent outbursts she may have had. It was one of the only times I can ever remember that she *actually* went through with an apology without finding some way to tie it back to my actions, or what I could've done differently.

That day I met up with my school counselor and cried for the first time in her office. I'm not exactly sure why - it just felt like the natural thing to do.

It was near the end of September when my mom left again. It was late, around 10:30 pm. A car was parked outside waiting for her. Summer had only just passed but it was cold, or rather *I* was cold. I wore shorts and a short sleeve shirt.

It's been a year but her scent still lingers. The smell of fresh coffee brewing and a cigarette bring me back to her each time.

I miss her, if you want to know the truth. I miss my mom so damned much.

DAVID ADELOWO

(NIGERIA)

WAS GIVING A PRESENTATION about my heritage, and panic started creeping in. I could see the condemnation on their faces - the stares that asked why I was so different. To an outsider, the small, black boys and girls that filled the sixth grade classroom would have all looked identical.

But I was a mistake and an oddity. I was black, but I was the wrong kind of black. I was worse than black.

I was African.

My family immigrated to the US when I was six years old, and my parents enrolled me in a local school, where I was introduced to a whole new way of learning. Some of my classmates were friendly, but others made fun of the way I talked or looked. I often got bullied for my accent, and my inability to say certain words properly (especially words that had the "th" sound, like three). I got called a "small African boy" every time my name was brought up in their conversations, which was rare.

My insecurities grew. I started to question my accent, my clothing choices, and sometimes even the texture of my hair, all of which marked me as African, and not African-American. Back in Africa, nobody cared about the clothes I wore, or the shoes I had on my feet. Here, my classmates bullied me for my light-up Sketchers and the multi-colored shoes my parents would buy me. I longed to blend in, to be just another face in the crowd, free from the burden of standing out. But the more I tried to fit in, the more I felt like an outsider.

One day, my teacher announced a heritage presentation project. Each student was tasked with sharing the unique aspects of their cultural background with the class. Panic set in as I considered the prospect of revealing my African heritage to a room full of kids who isolated me for who I was.

Despite my reservations, I decided to embrace the challenge. I spent nights researching - creating a visual masterpiece that showcased the rich history, traditions, and vibrant culture of Nigeria. On the day of the presentation, I stood nervously in front of the class, clutching my carefully crafted poster. As I began to speak, something happened. The tone of my voice changed, and my eyes lit up with passion. I spoke about the rhythmic beats of Nigerian music, the flavorful cuisine that tickled the taste buds, and the deep sense of community that permeated every aspect of life. To my surprise, the classmates who had once seemed so distant began to lean in, seemingly interested in my storytelling. At the end of my presentation, I felt like a burden was lifted off my shoulders. I felt like myself.

The next day, it was back to the regular schedule. To an outsider, the small black boys and girls that filled the sixth grade classroom would have looked identical.

It finally started to feel that way too.

RAFAELA CURA
(BRAZIL)

M Y MOM WOULD CALL me from the kitchen. "Sarah," she'd yell, as I came bounding down the steps in my perfect American clothes, ready for a perfect American day, my curly blond hair tied in perfect American pigtails.

I wanted it so badly sometimes I would hear it even when I wasn't dreaming. "Sarah," they'd say, instead of Rafaela. Rafaela, a name like a pasta shape, closer to a Ninja Turtle than an American Girl.

I resented my name and the culture it came from.

My extremely Brazilian name did not match with my face or this new life my parents had created for us. I would constantly hear "there is no way you´re Brazilian, you're way too white." To Brazilians, I was whitewashed, despite my fluent Portuguese. I heard it a lot of times from my grandfather. I couldn't open my mouth without hearing, "You can just tell you are speaking to a white person."

My name didn't help. My name was the name of a Brazilian, and I was growing up to be anything but.

Eventually, I decided to stop speaking Portuguese entirely and fully adopt English. If I was going to look white, and be told I speak white, then I was going to *be* white. My parents hated the fact that I would only respond in English from the simplest things they asked me.

"*Rafaela, não é 'yes,' você sabe disso!*"

"Yes," I'd say. "Yes."

As a teenager, my family and I moved to the Iron-bound section of Newark. I couldn't go to a bakery, or a park, without being fully immersed in my culture and my language. I felt disconnected. I couldn't unteach myself how to be "Sarah."

And so, my mother called me from the kitchen. "Sarah," she'd yell, as I came bounding down the steps in my perfect American clothes, ready for a perfect American day, my curly blonde hair straightened into a perfect American blowout. Yet this time I didn't have to pretend. This "Sarah" wasn't someone that I was wishing to be but someone I was.

All I'm missing is the name.

MELODY SANCHEZ

[SPAIN]

"No le digas a nadie. Mantenlo en secreto. Mantente a salvo."

We were on our way home from a party when my mother and I were hit by a careless driver - a small fender bender that, while disruptive to our day and certainly not welcome, was not something that should cause a crisis. A car trying to merge attempted to yield into traffic and hit our car. Nobody was hurt. We got out of the car, the other driver got out of hers. We exchanged apologies and "are you okays?" Then, somebody suggested calling the police. Panic came across my mother's face.

I don't think I really understood what being an undocumented immigrant meant until that moment.

By the time I got to high school, I understood all too well the struggles of being undocumented, particularly as my friends started applying to summer and college preparatory programs. I could never apply - for every twenty that our administrators shared, maybe one wouldn't ask for a social security number. Recently, I asked my guidance counselor about working papers. I thought maybe I could apply for a part-time job. I was wrong. Those nine digits have stood taller than any wall, and stronger. My family always told me to work hard at school so that I wouldn't end up in a factory, but there were times I felt helpless.

Ever since I can remember, my mom says a prayer when we get in a car, not for the safety of her passengers but to avoid the police, who she believes will ask for our papers. Late in his life, when my grandfather would get sick, he would avoid the doctor, as he wasn't able to apply for insurance. For nine years, from the time I arrived in this country, my family would refuse to let me get on a plane. Every day, we pray and hope that nobody catches us - shadow people under the bright glare of the American Dream.

Back at the car, my mom and I argue as we desperately ring my stepdad to figure out if we should call the police for our small accident.

"*¿Y si nos preguntan por nuestros papeles?*" my mom pleads, fear and panic in her eyes. Finally, she makes her decision.

"*No. No le digas a nadie*," she says. "Do not tell anyone. Keep it secret. Keep you safe."

JENNIFER PATRICIO
MELQUIADES

(BRAZIL)

W E WEREN'T READY TO leave behind our Brazilian roots. Instead, we chose to bring them along wherever life took us. Our new home was a blank canvas where we added the vibrant colors and the summery details of Brazil to our furniture, walls, pictures, carpets, plates, cups, and into the everyday moments to keep our culture alive.

"Mae, remember that first *Festa Junina* we had here?" I asked, the smell of grilling *picanha* in the air. She gave me her brightest smile.

"*Sim*! That improvised *quadrilha* party in our back-yard! It was like having a piece of Brazil right here with us."

Soon, our celebrations went beyond our home and began to involve our community. The smell of *picanha*, the pig's *linguiça,* and the soft bread that are in every Brazilian barbecue, *pão de alho,* became a nod to flavors from the homeland we could share; a tasty reminder of our roots that grew new branches in our neighborhoods. Our friends happily joined, becoming part of the Brazilian holidays and parties.

Even though we were not always able to celebrate the holidays with our traditions, we would always try to find something that is also a part of our tradition to do. Like the time we decided to wear white to express the wish for peace in the new year. Or how the samba, like a heartbeat, would echo through our parties and bring them to life, opening a portal from the streets of Newark to those of Rio Grande do Norte.

In this faraway place, away from the vibrant streets of our Brazilian home, we filled our homes with colors as vibrant as the Brazilian flag.

Ever since I arrived in the United States, I noticed my culture only lived within my family and not in everyone that I was surrounded by.

It's been our mission - and joy - to change that.

TREASURE POOLE

(HAITI)

M Y MOM AND DAD weren't together by the time I was born. My mom moved on especially fast, and I can't say I minded because I loved having a step-father. He already had four sons by the time he met my mother, so "Majo" took me in with open arms as his only daughter. That first year I moved to America - when I was five - was the loneliest year of my life, so I was happy to have an adult who cared.

Coming to America from Haiti was not difficult, but it was confusing. I was confused about why my mom wouldn't let me go outside alone at night, and confused about why everyone could afford *atik liksye yo* like cars and glass windows. Everytime I asked about the differences I was told by my mother or grandmother, "*li pa gen pwoblèm m okipe.*" It doesn't matter. By shutting me out, they taught me to stay silent, and they taught me so well that I continued to struggle learning to communicate.

It was somehow worse in school. The charter school I went to was so big, the first time I saw it I thought it had to be a mansion. My first day, I had to see the lady in the big office with glass everywhere, and when I spoke, I knew she couldn't understand.

My school had no special support for non-English speakers so I had to attend a so-called normal class. Each week, my mother would print a list of phrases that my teacher could use to help me learn the English meanings of: *liv* meant book and *chèz* meant chair. I felt proud to learn, however slowly, but also offended. The way my teacher taught me words made me feel like a dog being taught to sit.

I felt so small. My teacher would ask me questions but I didn't know how to answer, or in what language, or in a way that gave her what she wanted while staying true to myself and my reality. I answered. Or tried to. I kept stuttering and putting my head down, thoughts in Creole and English simultaneously rattling around my head. I left a part of myself in Haiti, a part I couldn't find in America.

I felt torn and confused, not knowing who I really was or where I really belonged.

No doubt because of this, and despite the language barrier, my step-father and I bonded quickly. I learned about all of his family's culture, and the things he personally enjoyed. I drove around in cars that bounced with fancy rims, and listened to loud, vulgar music. I couldn't understand the words but it didn't matter; I didn't need to understand to know that we were connecting. I needed so desperately to have any kind of connection, and my step-father filled a gap where my mom and grandmother and classmates might have been instead.

My step-dad stole cars and hung out with people who were involved in similar activities. I didn't know any of this at the time - I just knew he smelled nice and gave me money and all his friends did the same thing. My birth father was a *vakabon* too, but not because he was into any crime, just in the sense that he was kind of broke. But you don't need money to make a kid happy. We would take the lightrail to NYC and walk around, and he would take me to parks around his house. I was so happy being with my dads. When they focused on me, they made me feel like I belonged. And that was everything I ever wanted.

One day, I was getting ready to go back home to my mom, and I went to give my dad a kiss. He quickly pulled me off of him. I was confused. He asked me who taught me to kiss like that because I tried to use my tongue. I don't know why. My father says I told him "Majo does it."

My father told my mother this and she insisted he was lying. My mother told me that my father hated her because she had moved on. She told me he was crazy and that I shouldn't listen to him. My dad would say things that felt even worse:

"Your mom doesn't love you."

"She let someone hurt you."

"She's just trying to take you away from me."

I didn't know who to believe.

The courtroom I went to was so big, the first time I saw it I felt like it had to be a mansion. I had to see the judge in the big office with glass everywhere, and when I spoke, I knew he couldn't understand.

I felt so small. My mom was on one side and my dad on the other. My mom was crying. The judge asked me questions but I didn't know how to answer, or in what language, or in a way that gave everybody what they wanted while staying true to myself and my reality. I answered. Or tried to. I kept stuttering and putting my head down.

"Do you want to live with your mom or dad," he asked.

Thoughts in Creole and English rattled around in my head. I wanted both, to *be* both. The judge told me I had to choose.

I felt torn and confused, not knowing who I really was or where I really belonged.

PART FOUR

JOURNEY'S END TO A NEW BEGINNING

HE YELLS OUT, "¡QUE VIVA MI PAÍS!" AND THE REST SHOUT, "¡QUE VIVA!"

HE SCREAMS, "¡QUE VIVA MI FAMILIA!" AND WE ALL SCREAM BACK. "¡VIVA!"

YEWANDE HAMZAT

(NIGERIA)

I N THE BACK OF a first grade classroom, the heavy choco-late flavor of the Milo Cubes sat sweetly on my tongue. I had stuffed about fifteen of them into the pocket of my navy blue sweater, and worked my way through one by one; silently unwrapping the thick green paper and popping the brown cubes into my mouth. Although it wasn't the designated snack time, I knew I could eat in peace, since my teacher would avoid calling my name as much as they possibly could. Yewande means "My mother has returned," in Yoruba, but in English, it meant an awkward chuckle and a "I might not get this right."

I'd be a liar, though, if I said I wanted to use my American name like so many kids in my church had. Even with my near-perfect English - which my parents enforced to ensure I would succeed in the country they fought so hard to have me in - to offer my sister a "*pele*" when she coughed, or an "*ese*" to my aunties and uncles when they prayed for me, brought me warmth. The comfort of belonging to something ancient - of knowing that the grandmother I would never get to meet, who had never stepped foot in America, had always been watching over me - reassured me when I felt lost in America. And most of all, the sweet taste of a Milo Cube, brought in hordes by my father from Nigeria.

It's not like I didn't want to share - my companionship or my cubes. I just didn't think it was worth it to be stared at like an alien whenever I spoke. In the face of an unfamiliar language, I stuttered and whispered and wished so deeply to be back home.

Eventually, I resigned to eating the cubes in the back of the class.

One day, my seat partner noticed my secret eating, and when a first grader sees the possibility of candy, they won't hesitate to seek it out.

"What's that?"

"It's Milo candy. From Nigeria."

"Oh…"

"…"

"…"

"Do you want some?"

I sat, laser-focused on my seat partner's hands as they unwrapped the green paper, revealing the powdery cube inside. They held it in their hand for a while, and then popped it in their mouth whole.

One hard bite. A tentative chew. Then a more confident one. Then, their eyes lit up and they turned to me as they exclaimed, "These are really good, Yewande!"

The pronunciation was a bit off, muffled by their full mouth - but they tried. That was all it took. The taste of Milo Cubes, my presence, was accepted in America.

It was the sweet taste of chocolate. And a new home.

WINIGA BATOMA

(TOGO)

B ACK IN MY COUNTRY of Togo, in the schools, we used
to get flogged. If you did something bad, they would
flog you. If you got bad grades, they would flog you. This
was expected as a necessary means of education. Even
parents flogged their children at home.

The thought of this punishment was always in the
back of my mind.

"Winiga," my dad would say, lounging in his chair
with the TV news on, his towel held threateningly in
his hand, "bring your grades up or you're going to get
flogged." He was a direct man, and his word was ironclad.

Four years ago, I came to America and life is very
different now.

There was this one time in school when I got a bad
grade and I thought I was going to get flogged.

My teacher gave me back a bad grade in math. I
inhaled sharply and froze. I waited. And waited. But

nothing happened. The teacher, instead of hitting me, simply continued the class. I exhaled slowly, the stress melting away.

In America, they said there were many freedoms. The one I like most is the freedom to fail.

KIWENDSIDA OUEDRAOGO

(BURKINA FASO)

THEY WERE CONVINCED IT was a disease, a rash that swallowed my hand whole, a red infection starting at my fingertips, twisting to my fingers and engulfing my palm.

I had only been in the United States for three months, knew very little English, and was terrified of being the outcast at my new school. Most days I said little and walked down the hall with my head down, trying desperately to avoid all human interaction. This day, my teacher's screams made me the center of attention whether I wanted to be or not.

"What's on your hand?" She grabbed me by the arm and pulled me into the classroom. I didn't know what to say.

"Oh, she's the new kid. She doesn't speak English," someone else said.

"Look at her hand!" the teacher exclaimed.

"Oh my God! What is that?" the other said, frightened at the sight.

"I don't know. I just saw that her hand was like that," the teacher replied, holding my arm as if it were on fire.

"What do we do?"

"Maybe it can come off with soap!"

"Child, speak to me," the teacher said, "I know you don't speak but try to explain what happened to your hand."

Not knowing how to respond, I remained silent.

"Are you sick? Is that it? Nod your head yes, or shake no!"

"Someone call the nurse!"

Had they asked me in French, I could have explained without all the fuss. In my home country, Burkina Faso, Africa, we call it *jabbi*. Others might call it *mehndi*. In America, the intricately designed body art is known simply as henna.

Traditionally, the practice of henna is used mostly during Ramadan. My mom is especially experienced in this tradition.

My grandmother ships the dry henna directly from Africa along with the tape needed to complete the designs.

My mom then takes the dry henna, puts it in a bowl, and pours water on it until it looks like mud, leaving it to soak for an hour or two before cutting out the tape patterns.

I would ask my mom to cut the tape into thin, long pieces so it can be swirled onto my fingers one way and sometimes the opposite way, making little rhombuses on my fingers. Sometimes, I write out my initial on the palm of my hand.

After that's done, I have to soak my arm in water to help the henna stick. When the palm of my hand and the back of my fingers are filled, my mother has me gently close my fist with my thumb in, not quite like how you might throw a punch but not altogether different. Then a plastic bag gets tied around my hand, making me appear and feel silly. The next day, my mother unwraps the bag and, soon, the beauty of the henna starts to show. My mom would remind me to put shea butter on my hands to keep it moisturized and shiny.

Back in the classroom, my teachers were still debating what to do with my arm.

"Is that blood," one yelled, disgusted. I looked down, watching as my teacher held my wrist as if I were contagious.

Bewildered, we both looked from my hand to hers. From hand to hand, and back again. I had just arrived in America, and already we disagreed on which one held the true disease.

DAMIAN TAMAY

(ECUADOR)

I N ELEMENTARY SCHOOL, I had a math teacher who really helped me, even though she knew I could not speak English. For me, she was the best teacher because she used to be so patient with me. She didn't think I wasn't smart because I couldn't do the work in two languages, and she would translate it sometimes into Spanish so I could finish.

On the day my graduation arrived, I had to go to my school to pick up my diploma because I graduated virtually. When I got to the school, she saw me and gave me a hard hug and, when I was about to leave, she called me and gave me an envelope.

When I got home I opened it and there was a letter inside. I took the letter out and started reading. The letter was not too long, just a few words. I couldn't believe she wrote the letter in Spanish!

"*Te voy a extrañar mucho,*" it said. "*Gracias por todo, y nunca tengas miedo de hablar y decir lo que sientes.*"

After I read the letter I felt something in my heart, a feeling that would make me cry. She wrote all that because she knew I was shy during class and I was a quiet student. I know she wrote that to motivate me.

I still have that letter stuck on the wall. It means a lot to me because every time I read it I remember her, and also remember those times she taught me even though I did not know English.

"I'm going to miss you a lot, thank you for everything," Ms. Singley wrote. "Never be afraid to speak up and say what you feel!"

Thank you, I say to her now. I will share my voice with the world. I don't think I will be afraid.

DANIELLA OYEMONLAN

(NIGERIA)

HAD NEVER SEEN MY mother cry.

I didn't see her cry during the nearly fourteen hour flight from Nigeria to America. I didn't see her cry a single day while we stayed in Maryland and had to share a small room in the big house that belonged to our family friend. I didn't see her cry when she found out our immigration court date had been pushed back for the third year in a row.

Her eyes remained dry through the long, grueling hours that she had to work overnight while also taking classes during the day, all while ensuring that my brother and I made it to school, and that we were fed, clothed and happy. Her eyes remained dry throughout every holiday, when she would be confronted again and again that what she could provide wasn't up to our expectations. She was stoic every Christmas we couldn't afford a tree, let alone presents to put under them.

It wasn't until we moved into our first real house that I began to notice the cracks in her facade. We all lived together - I had my own room, my brother had his, and my mom shared the master with my step-father. The bright orange walls, although ugly, brought comfort. Knowing I had the privilege of my own room gave me enough happiness to forget about the problems we had as a family.

In African households, there is no such thing as abuse, there is only discipline. I lived in a very African household. When my step dad entered the picture, yelling and long lectures turned into slaps and hits. A missing phone, laptop or remote control was replaced with belt marks and red watery eyes.

Conflict was very common and every time, my mother ended up in the middle - my brother and I on one side, my step-father on another. I saw her neutrality as taking *his* side, and I often wished she would just tell my step dad to leave.

One day while my aunt was visiting from Nigeria, everything erupted. My mom has told me I've always had a hot head, and it boiled over in anger at my step-father. During the argument, tears flooded from our eyes one by one. First my aunt, then me, and lastly, finally, my mother. It was the first time I'd seen her cry and her tears spoke volumes. She cried the longest and the hardest. I immediately went to comfort her, her sadness fueling mine.

"*Pèlé*" was all I could repeat to her. It was the only Yoruba word I knew at the time and the only thing I could think of that would comfort her in any way. It was a different kind of hurt seeing her lose control.

Later that night she told us that when I was very young, and she was still facing abuse from my biological father, she gathered the courage to leave only when I yelled at him to stop. I was just two years old, and her pain as the abuse turned on me fueled her rage. She showed me photos of long ago memories as proof, long forgotten times since we boarded the plane to America.

I looked at her and understood what would come next. Until that night, I had never seen my mother cry. But, then, she is an African and an immigrant - it is not in her nature to cry for herself.

BRIANNA AGUILAR

(MEXICO)

O NCE UPON A TIME there was a young girl who hated her body. It seemed that everywhere she looked, there was hair growing—on her arms, her legs, even hair connecting her eyebrows. But the one that bothered her the most was the patch of hair above her upper lip. The young girl thought this was not something young girls should have, and hated it and herself.

It started when she was exactly eight years old. The classroom was noisy with the students' loud chatter that bounced throughout the room. Each student was obligated to do a math worksheet. While the majority of the children worked on the assignment, many did not. She sat with a group of students who joked, fooled around, and ignored the sheet of paper that lay in front of them. One of the girls in the group had been quietly observing the young girl as she spoke. She tilted her head in disgust as she gazed at her peer. She began to whisper to the classmate near her, and that classmate whispered to another. It continued on until it reached the boy on the left side of the young girl. Curiosity got the best of the young girl and she decided to ask, "What is everyone talking about?" But the observing girl burst into laughter and pointed to the young girl's upper lip.

"Look," she exclaimed. "She has a mustache!"

The other kids giggled and called her, "The mustache girl!"

The young girl felt her face flush with embarrassment. Touching her top lip, she felt ashamed and disgusted. She tried to speak out, to defend herself, but the young girl felt a knot in her stomach, and as soon as she opened her mouth all that came out was unintelligible murmurs. Her lips quivered, and she forced herself to focus on her black shoes that were beneath the table. The feeling of being judged and discriminated against became stronger as she began to hear other kids whisper about how she must've been a boy in disguise.

The young girl tried to hold back the tears. But, then, she couldn't hold them back any longer. A single tear rolled down her cheek, followed by another and another. Her shoulders shook as she tried to hold back her sobs, but it was no use. Her classmates' words were like daggers, poking and prodding at her sensitive heart.

"Boohoo, mustache girl," one of her classmates mocked. The young girl's sobs turned into hiccups and chokes as she tried to speak. All she wanted was for the ground to open up and swallow her whole.

For a few years after that day, the young girl would look at herself in the bathroom mirror every chance she could get and would sob into the sink. All she would see is the 'mustache girl,' that 'boy in disguise.'

The young girl's mother began to notice how her daughter was acting. She noticed how the young girl would touch her face, mainly on her upper lip area where the mustache grew. One day when the girl got ready to leave the house to go to a small shop in town, she stepped into the bathroom to once again look at her hair. She frowned and began to tear up. Her mother walked through the hallway, just in time to pass by the bathroom where she heard the murmurs of the young girl. She knocked on the door and stepped inside.

"Why do you look at yourself the way you do?"

The young girl had never discussed her insecurity with her mother before. But something about the way her mother looked at her made her want to open up. She took a deep breath and poured her heart out. The young girl told her mother about the mustache, the taunts from her classmates when she was younger, and her feelings of not belonging.

The young girl bit her lip, unsure of what would come next. Her mother looked at her with a small, soft smile, and putting a hand on her daughter's shoulder, she spoke again.

"You know, in Mexico being hairy is actually considered a beautiful thing. Not *too* hairy of course, but it's a beauty standard!"

The young girl looked at her mother and sighed.

"You're just trying to make me feel better," the young girl muttered, lowering her chin.

"Take a look at Frida Kahlo! Her eyebrows were connected, and she had a small mustache that she actually embraced and celebrated. She's an icon of beauty and strength," the young girl's mother said. "Just like you!"

Before the young girl could answer, her mother continued, "Julia Pastrana? She was a dancer. Her face and body was covered with straight black hair. Do you know what people would call that woman? They'd say she was 'dog-faced', the 'hairy woman,' and 'ape-faced' just because of how much body hair she had. But eventually, she was considered one of the most beautiful women in Mexico. You're everything those women would want to be."

The young girl nodded, completely speechless. She thought about how amazing her culture was, and how lucky she was to have such a beautiful mom.

For the first time in a long time, the young girl thought maybe she was beautiful, too.

JHON SALAZAR

(DOMINICAN REPUBLIC)

REMEMBER THE FIRST DAY I met my father, because it was the day I first came to America. I had never been on a plane before and it was all too much for me – the hum of the engines, the bright lights, the speed of this new world – all of it was overwhelming and terrifying. I woke up as they were getting me out of the car.

I had never met my father – he had moved to America before I was born – but there he was, standing next to my uncle in front of this strange and massive house. I fell into his giant arms, and he took me into the basement, a tiny room underground where I would spend the next few years of my life. The first thing I remember – the first thing I really remember in this new country and with this new person – was gently falling asleep as he carried me out of the darkness and into the house.

A couple months later I was enrolled into elementary school and it was tough. Not only for the typical reasons of language and culture shock, but because of the bullying I was the victim of almost immediately. It didn't help that my first language was not English, which only exacerbated the already growing difficulty I was having in connecting to my peers. I started to develop anger issues, and would act out, desperate for someone to help. One day in class we were playing a game when I got very excited. My teacher thought I was about to have a fit, so she called someone from the office.

There was a loud knocking on the door of the classroom and the door opened to the sight of a man outside. He was tall and menacing, and I was scared as he pointed his finger at me, insisting that I follow him to go "meditate." He brought me to an empty room, showed me a pose, and told me to hold it with my eyes closed. I was quiet and did as he instructed. Eventually, I opened my eyes to find he had left the room and shut off the lights. It was pitch black and I was locked in. I was scared and began to panic, and the more I got worked up, the more alone I felt. I slammed at the door, my fists punching into the metal - but there was nobody around to save me.

Two hours later they opened the door. They had forgotten I was there. My eyes took forever to adjust to the light, but I told nobody for fear of going back. I became much quieter after that.

A couple weeks later I was transferred to a new school, where I had a very kind teacher that looked after me as if I was her son. She was an immigrant too and had also come from the Dominican Republic. I met a kid who was also bullied a lot and we ended up becoming great friends. He helped me get my voice back.

Years later, as I was telling this story to my mother, remembering that far away day I was locked in a room, I would learn that it was my father who pushed for me to be in a new school.

It made sense. That's what fathers do: They pick you up. They pick you up in their giant arms, and they carry you out of the darkness.

HAZIQ SAJJAD

(PAKISTAN)

M Y UNCLE WAS EXCITED to share the news.

"Haziq," he said. "I applied for your citizenship. These are the questions and you need to practice."

He handed me a study guide full of facts about America, the Constitution and the amendments, the holidays and history. I tried learning by myself, but I'm not great at reading and I didn't know American History. I was at a new school and decided to ask a teacher to help me, so after my history class I asked my teacher, Ms. Famosi, if she would help me study for my citizenship test.

The first day we met she Googled the test and printed out the questions for me. She had me try to read the questions to see how my English was. It was OK. The next time we made flashcards for all 100 questions. Everyday I would go into class and ask, "Ms. Famosi today we study after school?" I was thinking about the test so much. We practiced 3-4 days after school each week. One day when

I went home, my uncle quizzed me and he said this is good, keep trying in school.

My teacher told me, "Haziq, when you leave the school you need to do a little bit of studying on your own" so I downloaded an app so I could keep learning about America. When summer came I did not practice much because I had a job, but when I got my schedule for junior year I saw I had Ms. Famosi again and I said "this is good." She told me she would start tutoring me again after school. The first time back we did a practice and it turned out I remembered a lot of the questions, but we needed to practice my reading and writing. The reading and writing part of the test I needed the most help with.

A full year after my uncle first told me to study, my interview was scheduled. I told Ms. Famosi and she was very excited for me. I was nervous and didn't know what it would be like so we watched a video on what to bring and what to expect.

After a year of practicing the date finally approached. They called my name, and I showed them my passport and green card. I went into the room, powered off my phone, and gave the oath.

"I swear to tell the truth, the whole truth and nothing but the truth," I said.

The officer asked me three questions and after answering them all right, the lights started blinking and shut off. She took a long time on the computer and finally told me something about how the system had broken and I needed to reschedule. I was sad and crying. I called my uncle and he picked me up. He said there was nothing we could do.

After this I went back to studying after school and checking my citizenship and immigration status everyday. A week or two later after checking everyday the portal said they would call for an interview, meaning my progress was lost and I had to go back to the start.

All in all, it's been a year of hard work, yes, and kindness. But also a year of bureaucracy and failure, and confusion and frustration for me as I try to do the right thing in the right ways but get pushed down.

But, then, it's been a full year of learning about America.

GABRIEL DO CARMO

(BRAZIL)

U PON COMING TO AMERICA, my dad was always surrounded by people who spoke a language he couldn't understand. This was a struggle because he couldn't do much in America without speaking English, and relying on other people to translate was unreliable and tedious. His salvation would come, he knew, when my twin brother and I were born. To have a child that was born in America and would learn the native language would be a blessing - a translator who would always be near when you needed them, eager to please, and simple to understand. To have two such blessings was just good fortune.

He still couldn't speak one word of English. He would take us to the park, and watch us as we slid, swung, and bounced to the tune of American words. But he could never communicate with us or the other adults in the language we screamed and laughed and played in.

At home, however, the blessings of twin infants became apparent. Often, before bed, my brother and I would watch cartoons. Soon, my dad began to join us. Almost immediately it became a ritual. Anytime we watched a show or movie, my dad would switch the audio to English and turn on English subtitles. It became a daily commitment for him to fully immerse himself in understanding the language.

As my brother and I joined him in watching a cartoon called *Courage the Cowardly Dog*, it turned into an interactive language-learning experience. Taking the first baby steps into the new language, my dad would quote the show, leaning forward and mimicking the main character:

"There's something going on here or my name is Stinky Lulu," he'd say in a funny accent. "And thank goodness it's not!"

The room burst into giggles, mainly because the accent was very funny, and eventually, those small leaps into communication would become running gags, embedded in our movie evening rituals. After that, my dad would casually break out into Courage the Cowardly Dog's Stinky Lulu line whenever something suspicious happened.

Over time, movie nights became an essential part of our daily routine. What began as a way to learn a language evolved into a family tradition. It was more than just learning the language; it was also about the family bond we developed while going through this learning experience together. As the subtitles became less necessary, and the need for explanations were no longer needed, it was evident that my dad had conquered the language barrier through his unconventional approach.

All his adult life, my dad struggled to learn English. In the end, though, all it took were his two sons.

And a little Courage.

XEIDA ARCE

(PERU)

E VERY TIME THE WORDS "I'm Hispanic" came out of my mouth, it felt like a lie.

When I was with friends, I felt like an outsider. They were fluent in Spanish, ate traditional food, and listened to Spanish music frequently. I knew enough Spanish to hold a conversation, ate traditional foods only on holidays and special occasions, and listened to American rap and R&B. I felt like a fraud.

When my grandma came from Peru, all she knew was Spanish. My mom is the same – she grew up in an ethnic community surrounded by other first-generation immigrants and learned the language of her ancestors before she could read or write her English ABCs. In contrast, by the time I was eight, I could barely understand the Spanish muppet on *Sesame Street*.

I still feel like I'm not Spanish enough. When I go shopping, people ask me for help in Spanish and I can only understand so much. When I speak to family in my grandmother's native country, I can't have a conversation with them. For a long time, the best I could do was say "*Hola*," awkwardly smile, and walk away.

The first time I went to Peru was an exercise in rapid-fire gibberish.

"*¿Cómo está todo en tu vida? ¿Todo bien?*"

"*¿Tienes novio? ¿Qué haces ya en los Estados Unidos?*"

"*¿Cómo están las escuelas?*"

It was basic, Spanish 101, *Dora the Explorer* "*Yo soy Dora*," level stuff. And it went right over my head. I spent the whole trip barely talking. I just watched everyone else laugh with each other as I sat in the corner in silence. I was there with these people but I was somewhere else.

After that trip, I told myself I would practice Spanish so I could communicate better. I decided to practice with my Peruvian grandma. In return, I let her practice English with me. We would start with the basics:

"*¿Cómo está tu día?*"

"*Estabas bien?*"

"*¿Comiste?*"

"*Si*"

"*¿Bañaste?*"

"*Si*"

It's gotten better. Recently, without realizing it, we transitioned to full-blown debates, closer now to an actual conversation than the first day at Spanish I. My grandma and I can laugh now. I feel like I finally belong.

'*Hoy va a ser un gran día,*" I tell her.

"*Estoy bien, estoy feliz.*"

"*Yo soy hispana.*"

JAYLENE GONZALEZ

(PUERTO RICO)

M Y GRANDMOTHER IS A miracle.

My grandmother was born in Puerto Rico and given the name Nydia Milagros. Milagros means miracle in Spanish. But, even though she was named miracle, she had everything but miracles in her life. She grew up terribly poor with an abusive step-father and a mother who was just as scared of him as the children were.

Too happy? She got beaten.

Too sad? She got beaten.

The only times she was tolerable was when she was invisible.

The first time I heard this story, it felt familiar, reminding me of my own life.

Too happy? I got yelled at.

Too sad? I got yelled at.

The only times when it felt like I was tolerable was when I was invisible.

I couldn´t understand her; how could she speak so poorly about her childhood and incorporate so much of it into mine?

Last year, the day of my great-grandmother's funeral, I saw my grandmother cry for the first time. Something in that moment allowed me to see through the disguise, the protection, and the hurt. I didn't see the person she always pretended to be cry; I saw that scared little girl back in Puerto Rico cry. For the first time, I wasn't sad, confused, or angry with her. I felt pity, and in that pity, I understood her. And for that moment we both cried, sharing emotions, loudly, publicly, *visibly*.

She never apologized for what she had done, but she started to act differently, and that has allowed me to forgive her. Even after that day I saw more glimpses of my grandmother than I did the mask she always wore. Today I told my grandmother I loved her. She looked me in the eyes and smiled.

"I love you more, Jaylene."

My grandmother is a miracle.

But so am I.

ERICK VILLACIS

(ECUADOR)

M Y MOTHER INTERRUPTED MY dinner to tell me the bad news.

"Your aunt Monica is coming from Ecuador," she said. "I will be paying for them and for their transportation here." Though not stated, the implication is clear: this is money that we might need, and won't get back.

I'm baffled and unreasonably upset. "Why do we need to pay to help them?" I ask. "Can't they just arrive on their own?"

My mother goes quiet, but is waiting for me after dinner in the living room. She calls me over to the couch. Her pull, like gravity, is inescapable.

My mother's journey to America began when she was just 18, she explains, when she left Ecuador with the help of her brothers who were already living in the United States. She walked across the Mexican desert with nothing but a can of beans, a gallon of water, and a piece of bread; not knowing whether or not she would live to see the other side. But, she could never have taken that first step if it wasn't for the support of her family.

With family here, she had a goal to look forward to, and a shoulder to lean on. When she needed help, she went to family. When she needed advice, she went to family. When she needed money or shelter or prayer, she had her brothers to help. Family being present kept my parents going, no matter what obstacles came their way.

Now that my parents are situated, my mother says they are able to return the favor. With my Aunt Monica ready to take the journey, she will be welcomed with open arms. At minimum, my parents will help pay her way as she figures out her own life, just as my parents were once themselves gifted. Once embraced, my mother will extend her arms to embrace others.

I feel bad now and apologize to my mother, before turning to the picture we have of the Virgin de Guadalupe.

That night, I imagine a line of immigrants, and my uncles are part of it, and my mother and father are part of it, and I'm part of it, and my Aunt Monica is now part of it too. In my vision, everybody is reaching out to help the next person, each one extending a hand, arms outstretched, until it's a chain of helpers that cover the whole world and has no beginning and no end.

MANYAMA KEHMOR MARA

(LIBERIA)

"THANK YOU FOR CALLING Optimum. Please continue to hold and a representative will be with you soon. Your estimated wait time is 35 minutes."

Since the age of six I've been handling the business of my family. As the eldest daughter of an African home, I was used to handling all calls and knew the information for each member of my family like the back of my hand. I've been calling companies and pretending to be my mom since I was able to read the ingredients on a juice box. I have called bill collectors, customer representatives, and service industry care specialists. I've written letters to the welfare office and filled out applications and money orders to the rental office. Being the eldest daughter meant that instead of listening to the radio when I was younger, I memorized account numbers and birthdays.

I would always make sure to put on my "grown-up" voice.

Some days, when I'd go to school and hear that the other kids would get rewarded for good grades and test scores, I would be shocked. When I told my mom about my grades, she'd hit me with a "Good job." The good grades continued to roll in, but she couldn't be less impressed. If I came home with an A, she'd ask, "*Plus ye min?*"

As a child who strived for acceptance and validation, I was hurt. I wanted the celebration that the other kids received. But as the daughter of an African mother, an A wasn't enough.

"You don't have a reason to fail," she'd say.

My mother's attitude seemed to make perfect sense to her, but yet my heart began to grow weary of the childhood I never had.

I grew tired of putting on my grown-up voice.

The hold music from the phone begins again, drawing out my thoughts.

"Thank you for calling Optimum. Please continue to hold and a representative will be with you soon. Your estimated wait time is 34 minutes."

JUAN CAICEDO

(COLOMBIA)

FOUR MONTHS AFTER WE arrived in Newark, my mom and I went to the emergency room because she had a strong pain in her heart. Only recently in America, and a stranger to the language, I was terrified both because of her condition and because I was worried something would happen that I couldn't understand, or communicate. I thought back to a doctor in Colombia who pulled me aside and shared a diagnosis that needed no translation:

"Your mom will maybe die today," he said. "And there's no one here to help you."

I've been scared of every medical appointment since.

For me, it is sometimes hard to understand medical terms in Spanish. Now I was being forced to learn the language of medicine at the same time I was learning English to be able to facilitate translation between the many doctors, nurses, and hospital staff and my mother. Over the years, my mother has had a lot of procedures for her health, and I have been there for most of them, sometimes with my older brother, and sometimes by myself. There have been stressful moments when I have had to connect ideas in three languages to facilitate her care: milligrams, and pills, and hours, and routes, and pharmacies, and future appointments, and side-effects, and allergies.

The first big test came when my mother had to go to the hospital for nuclear therapy for her thyroids, and I was not able to go with her because it was dangerous for someone my age. They gave her two pills, but she got sick later at home. Sometimes my big brother would sleep at the house, but some days he would be forced to be away from her. On those days, we had to use video calls. I would talk to her, and try to use my voice to calm her.

I remember a lot of white rooms with bare walls.

After procedures to save her life, we would get bills in the mail, bills that needed repayment if we hoped to get service the next time she was in trouble. My mom, looking at the many zeros, would get disheartened, and sometimes say it might be better to not go for treatment. However, thanks to a friend, my mother was able to receive charity, especially important because, due to her condition, she cannot work. We started filling our calendar with all the appointments we could now go to worry-free. She got echocardiograms, electrocardiograms, full hemograms, respiratory panels, thyroid hormones

(T3-T4-TSH), nuclear procedures for hyperthyroidism, and other procedures with more complicated names that I was barely able to remember let alone translate.

I remember my mother's eyes, the way they would crease, the way they looked wet, and would sometimes empty. And the way they sometimes wouldn't, full to the brim but not over.

Recently, I experienced the fear of seeing my mother undergo heart surgery. As she did, the words that had been following me from Colombia came back to me.

"Your mom will maybe die today," he said. "And there's no one here to help you."

However, the support provided by this country was exemplary. Every single doctor and nurse knew what was happening and could explain it. Somehow, over time, I got better at understanding English and medicine, and the change happened so imperceptibly that I never questioned it when I was finally at peace.

Before the surgery, my mom turned to me.

"*Te amo*," she whispered. "*No tengas miedo. Estoy bien.*"

Five hours later, she emerged from a successful surgery.

But of course she did. Her heart is strong.

And she has me to help her.

MICHAEL ADELEKE

(NIGERIA)

WAS BORN IN NIGERIA, into a family of wealth, and all the privilege that wealth afforded. I was driven by hired help to the most prestigious private school in my state, where I learned both Yoruba and English, and came home to a house full of "helpers" who would react to my every desire. We had lots of cars in our compound and would travel several times a year.

My bubble was both innocent and consistent, until I was forced one day to switch suddenly to homeschooling. Despite, or maybe because of my wealth, I was never the best at making friends, so the switch to homeschooling didn't affect me as much as it might have. But I was soon affected, when over the next several months, the staff in our house shrank until no one was left. To mirror this shift, our garage, once full of cars from every corner of the globe, became emptier and emptier.

My parents sat us down for a meeting and told us that what we had begun to notice was part of a process they had started months prior to move the family to the United States. They asked us to fast and pray together in honor of this new covenant, and told us this move was so that my siblings and I could have a richer future, full of even more opportunity. I knew immediately, of course, that they were lying.

The terrorist group Boko Haram - known primarily as the organization responsible for the mass kidnapping of 270 schoolgirls from Chibok - operated mainly in the northeastern part of my country, far removed from my own territory. Closer to home however, there was an even more frightening incident, a gruesome discovery known as the Ibadan Forest of Horror where Okada riders, a group of transportation bikers, formed a search party after one of their friends had gone missing. They came instead upon a ritualistic human trafficking den. The gruesome discovery included emaciated and malnourished survivors chained to walls, surrounded by a phalanx of human bones and viscera - skulls sunk into freshly butchered body parts. An investigation revealed that the building had been in operation for more than ten years.

We were moving out of an abundance of fear and because our wealth afforded us the opportunity to do so when many others couldn't.

The day we arrived was a cold winter day; a humbling cold to children used to the African heat. My father's friend was supposed to meet us at the airport and drive us to the hotel, but was nowhere to be found when we landed. The long day gave way to a long couple of months as my family looked for housing, forced instead to stay in motels and temporary abodes. At some point, after traveling around for a couple months my father left to go back to Nigeria and never came back. Soon, my mother had to look for work to help her children survive.

The real adjustment, for me, was in school, where as a foreigner I was placed into English as a Second Language classes even though I knew the language better than many Americans. Just getting to and from school was difficult for me, with having to wake up on time, and then having to take two buses across town, all without the aid of a driver to help me. Worst of all, I began to get bullied for being an African. This bullying was exacerbated as my family's money started to run out and my appearance began to match the taunts. My shoes would be all types of messed up, and my clothes old and worn.

It was a surprise, one day, when I learned I could stand up for myself. It was even more of a surprise when I discovered, as if by accident, that I could stand up for other people. I became the bully's bully - the strongest and most vengeful of my grade.

This ability to help others was a privilege, and the first privilege I ever actually earned.

For many, coming to America is a chance for new opportunities, a wealth that would otherwise have forever been beyond their grasp.

For me, coming to America was an opportunity for poverty and humility. An opportunity, not to find a job or an education, but an opportunity, someday, to find myself.

SAARAH SHABAZZ

(TRINIDAD)

B Y THE TIME I was eleven, I could make curry chicken and roti with my eyes closed and one arm tied behind my back. The *tanties* made sure of it.

Every Thursday was my turn to prepare the food. Each time, while washing my hands, I would mentally set my *niyyah* to prepare this meal for the pleasure of my parents, which is a good deed.

I typically began by powdering my hands with flour, and sprinkling baking powder and salt into a big ball on the table. Then I would add water little by little to knead it into dough. Once it was firm, I would break it into small little circles, put a small amount of ghee into them individually, and cover each with a cloth to rise.

While the roti dough was rising, I would begin making the curry chicken, which my Tanti Zanifa typically prepared in advance.

I lit the fume of the stove and set it to medium, coconut oil bubbling to match my anticipation, both in harmony to allow the chicken to reveal its aromatic tapestry. While that simmered for half an hour I went back to the roti, individually rolled out the small balls of dough, and began to light the *tawa*.

The rhythmic sound of the pots simmering in unison would calm me, particularly as they paired so perfectly with the *Quran* playing in the background, a melodic symphony of peace. The roti was now puffed up and golden, so I would take the *dabla* to fold the corners together to *buss up shot*. I smiled as I individually placed each roti into a cloth.

I could not resist the allure of the spices brewing in the pot of curry. When no one was looking, I would sneak a taste. If I got caught , my defense was always the same: "*I des tasting it!*" This momentary act of rebellion was one of my favorite parts of cooking. The *tanties* knew better than to complain, aware that's how they grew up, generations of hands in their own pots of boiling grease.

Everyone would make their way to the kitchen, and we'd all eat together as laughter filled the air.

What I loved most about my home was that there was always a promising comfort meal that reminded us of the native country. The moment one of the girls stepped into the kitchen, it was a representation of their fierce hearts.

That's what food meant to us: love. It's why the fumes are so hypnotizing, why marriages last so long.

What's that saying?

The quickest way to a man's heart is through his stomach.

***

When I was 12, my mother presented me with a choice: I could continue to pursue my education or go the more traditional route and prepare for marriage.

A revelation of my cousin as a potential fit hung in the air. At the mention of his name, an unsettling feeling came over me, and my chest got heavy.

"What age would I be married off?" I asked.

"Fifteen," my mother said.

I understand that my mother's gaze bore a silent plea for me to venture into education - a silent appeal mirrored in the weight of *the look* she gave me.

I knew that the marital route wasn't a fit for me in just *three* years. I barely knew *myself*. My mind raced at the thought of someone else in my space, a strange man seeing me without my hijab and taking me away from my family.

My mother's worried eyes confronted me. I knew she was only asking because it's her obligation to honor my cousin's request, the *tanties'* cunning eyes watching her every move.

My dad often comforts me by the simple mention of the 21st Ayah of Surah Ar-Rum from the *Quran*.

He reminds me that Allah has already written my other half before I even stepped foot on the face of this world, so there's no need to rush or stress.

Until this mystery man and I cross paths, I'll continue to laugh off the requests for my hand. When we find each other, it will be effortless, inshallah.

And while I don't know what he'll look like or where he'll be from, I know one thing: He's going to *love* my food.

WILLIAM XILOJ

(GUATEMALA)

T HE DAY I ARRIVED at Tia Dunia's house I was shown my father's old bedroom.

It was dark and cold, and the floors and walls were made of concrete. The only furniture was a small hammock in the middle of the room. As I looked around I felt as though those cold, stone walls would suffocate me; the only movement - the soft sway of the hammock from a light breeze.

At that moment I could envision my own bedroom: soft laminated floors, my big bed with soft sheets full of pillows, and the feeling of warmth all around.

I was a greedy child who always wanted everything that was in front of me: Toys, games, gadgets - I wanted them all; and moreover, all to myself. I would ask my father for the newest gizmo. Inevitably, the answer was always "No."

In the small room, in the small house, in the small, nowhere town, in the backwaters of the backcountry he came from, I finally knew my father's "No" was never the problem.

I was.

The day I arrived back, he waited for me at the airport. When we met for the first time after two weeks, I could not control my emotions. I ran to him, grasping him tightly. Although he couldn't be there, I knew he understood what I had experienced.

"*Gracias Papa*," I said.

"*¡De nada, hijo!*" he answered back.

"Can you ever forgive me?"

"Yes, my son," he said.

He looked at me smiling with wet eyes.

"The answer is always yes."

FERDOUSI BEGUM

(BANGLADESH)

GAVE MY FATHER A hug for the first time when I was
probably fourteen or fifteen. I have never told him I
love him. He's never even seen me cry. We exchange brief
dialogue once or twice a week with most of it consisting
of the basics: "Have you eaten?" or "Did you get home?"

As an immigrant desperately trying to provide for his
family, my father works so hard and so much that at times
it feels like we don't live together. On the rare occasions
I do see him, all I can remember are his fragile body and
tired eyes. He works such long shifts that he collapses at
home without getting to spend time with me. He works
until he breaks and there is nothing left.

My father has worked so hard at being a father that
he had no time left to be a father—given so much that
he has nothing left to give.

It's always been like this.

The irony of being bilingual is that you know two languages but are somehow silent in both. In Bangla, I cannot speak of the American culture that I am immersed in. In English, half of my life experiences and knowledge is left uncommunicated for fear of not belonging. Outside of my house, I am American. I speak English, dress in Western clothing, and enjoy coffee. Inside my house, I am Bengali. I speak Bangla, dress in cultural clothing, and drink chai.

My parents, who only know one language, are silenced in every part of their lives.

While he worked night and day, I wondered why I never saw him. I used to ask my mom when he would come home but eventually got tired of the answer. At night, I would sleep on the couch so that he would be forced to pick me up and take me to bed. Eventually, I was told that I was getting too big for that and I should let my father relax.

I know my father and I love each other dearly, but we suffer too much in our silence to share a word of affection.

As a kid, I watched my family struggle. I saw my brothers and my parents fight each other over responsibilities and duties and then, eventually, I watched as they continued to fight each other because they had to fight those they loved in the absence of anyone else to blame for their suffering.

NICOLE VELEZ-OCAMPO

(ECUADOR)

W HEN I WAS THREE years old, my parents were worried about my development. They took me to the doctor frequently because I was speaking less than a regular child should be.

"*Solo dice 'agua'*," they told my doctor.

Nobody could explain why I didn't talk; I just didn't. I would stay quiet and zone out looking at the ceiling, as if I was simply doing so out of a stubborn refusal.

During the time of these tedious and excessive doctor's appointments, my mother attempted to enroll me into Pre-K at First Avenue Elementary School. After my mom collated and presented all my legal documents, it was time for me to take an entrance test to assess my basic cognitive skills and speech ability. I was too young to process much of what was happening, but my mom remembers that day fully. Mostly, she says, she still remembers the frown on the faces of the administrators after I finished the exam.

"*¿Perdone Señora, pero no piensa usted que tal vez sea muda su hija?*" one advised. "*Debería estar hablando mucho más a esa edad. Pero no se preocupe, hay opciones para niñas como ella.*"

For people who suspected me of being mute, the "options" were special education programs. My mom was not going to take those options and she was absolutely going to worry - special education programs didn't sit right with her culture or generation. Instead, my mom insisted that something be done. That's when I wound up in the doctor's office, who eventually assigned me to a speech therapist. "An *English* one," my mom demanded. I didn't even speak one language, but my mother would settle for nothing less than two.

I remember my speech therapist's visits vividly. She would come to my house for my treatment sessions and set up colorful figurines and objects on my table that I'd have to learn and recite the names of.

One time she put up a small rubber '*vaca*' and '*pollo.*' "That is a cow," she pointed to the black and white toy, "and that is a chicken."

I looked at them curiously and pointed to each one as I repeated their names.

"Cow. Chicken," I said with a tiny accent.

"Good job!" my therapist exclaimed.

Every time I answered a question or stated a sentence properly she'd give me a warm smile or a high five. She made me feel like I was the smartest little girl to ever exist. I was learning two languages at once: English from my speech therapy sessions and Spanish from my parents and, according to my therapist, I was a fast learner. After six months of treatment, my parents were beginning to miss my silence.

My mom decided after the six-month mark that it was time to try again. I remember the morning when I walked next to my mom to the Newark Public Schools Central Office where I was to be tested to see if I was really meant for an NPS standard education program. After assessing me, my speech abilities were declared to be up to par, and I was welcomed to First Avenue that school year. My mom was ecstatic. That day she made me my favorite food, *fideos verdes*, and my entire family celebrated their chatterbox.

It took me a little longer than most to begin talking.

My mom would probably tell you now that I never stop.

KHLOE LINTON
(JAMAICA AND LIBERIA)

"KHLOE, WHERE ARE YOU from?"

"Well, I'm Liberian on my mom's side and Jamaican on my dad's."

"Which side do you claim more?"

Today, I pick Liberia. In doing so, I can't help but feel I'm disregarding all the trials and tribulations my father endured coming to America. I disregard him navigating the world as a young black man entering a strange and inhospitable environment. Disregard his struggle of being alone, of doing what he had to do to get by. Disregard him falling into the wrong crowd and paying the debt of that his whole life.

"I'm from Liberia."

Today, I pick Jamaica. In doing so, I can't help but feel that means I'm disregarding what my grandma went through in Liberia. I disregard her being the pioneer that brought the rest of her family across oceans. Disregard her putting her family above everything. Disregard her keeping her faith even in her toughest times. Disregard the way she raised me.

"I'm from Jamaica."

For years on end that stayed my answer - to express the side of me that was familiar and acceptable to other people while completely erasing the other. Until one day my grandmother passed. It burned anytime I opened my mouth to speak about her. I stayed silent for so long, but the quieter I was, the more I seemed to forget: the way she sounded, the clothes she wore and even sometimes the way she looked.

I hated myself for this, and knew the only way out was to embrace the totality of it all - to never forget because I never let myself deny even a single part of myself. I am the sum total of all that came before me.

"Khloe, where are you from?"

"Well, I'm Liberian on my mom's side and Jamaican on my dad's."

"Which side do you claim more?"

"Both."

MELISSA MASACHE-RAMOS

(ECUADOR)

M Y FAMILY BOUGHT THE cans of *carioca* in February; spray foam in a myriad of bright, vibrant colors. It was Carnaval week, and the cans would play a part in one of our most fun traditions.

The whole family is there - a symphony of *primos*, and *hermanos*, and *amigos*. Soon, the gathering is transformed. A bag of flour is set on a table; chairs, blankets, and tables are set aside; and objects on the floor are put away. As everyone gets ready, the cans of *carioca* are handed out. Those who are old enough, and want to play, receive one can each. Those who did not wish to participate, go to hang out in another area until the games are finished.

Once everyone is in their place, the coast is clear for the bravest to shoot first.

"*¡Viva el Carnaval!*" they shout, shooting foam at their unsuspecting victim.

"*¡Viva!*" responds everyone else.

Soon, foam is being sprayed in every direction, covering the floor and people in a wet film. My strategy is to slip away, hide behind anyone I can, peek around corners like a sniper in a movie, and spray the foam as fast as I can. During these fun times people laugh, and yell, and howl as they lock onto their next target.

"*¡Venga aquí!*" someone shouts.

"*¡Ahí! ¡Vaya por ellos en vez de mi!*"

"Gotcha!" my brother shouts whenever he hits someone.

"*¡Te téngo!*" I shout back, spraying foam at him.

Flour is thrown every now and then onto people and the floor. No one is exempt from getting messy, and soon our clothes become covered. Lines of color spread from peoples' backs, to their chests, to their legs, their head, and hair - all of it soaking in color like a sponge. Only a few minutes pass but it feels like hours. It's now a competition to see who can last the longest with some spray left.

Eventually, there is no more foam left. Just as everyone stops, I remember the bag of flour on the table. It's gone! One of my relatives has it, and she has no mercy. She takes handfuls of flour and pours it onto the people around her. It is so fast, no one has time to escape. As everyone cleans the foam from their clothes and the furniture, bachata music begins to softly play in the background

As more songs are played, people become more enthusiastic. The songs get louder, voices even more so.

My dad shouts "*¡Que viva Ecuador!*" and everyone responds, "*¡Viva!*"

He yells out, "*¡Que viva mi país!*" and the rest shout, "*¡Que viva!*"

He screams, "*¡Que viva mi familia!*" and we all scream back, "*¡Viva!*"

ACKNOWLEDGEMENTS

S PECIAL THANKS FOR THE completion of this project must go first and foremost to Principal Darleen Gearhart, who helped develop this book and then worked tirelessly at each stage to manifest it by forging partnerships and clearing red tape. She is a leader who is always able to get what she wants - not simply because she is smart, and capable, and brave - but because what she always wants is to help and serve children. I am proud to have partnered with her to bring you this collection.

Many thanks to Newark Public Schools, particularly the Office of English Language Arts led by Jazleen Othman. Ms. Othman helped facilitate district-wide participation, and was vital in organizing an editing day where we were able to bring over 100 student authors to a central location for targeted story conferencing. Thanks of course to the entire Board of Education and, most especially, Superintendent Roger León - all of whom have helped to nurture and elevate student voices in Newark while providing opportunities for their narratives to be shared. This book would not have been possible without their foundational focus on empathetic learning.

Many thanks to John Abeigon and the Newark Teachers Union, who supported this project in their newsletters and on social media, and who support teachers every day with their advocacy.

Many thanks to the teams at East Side and Central High Schools led by Carla Nunes and Tara Fehr, respectively, who helped shepherd and guide students towards this project, and who spent an entire day with me talking to kids and translating their narratives.

Thank you to the many teachers from all across Newark who shared this opportunity with their students, inviting them to be open and vulnerable with someone they've never met. Thanks in particular to Claudia Ferreira and Nicole Torres who worked with me and their students as translators, able to be smarter in three languages than I am in one.

Special acknowledgement is owed to my team at Science Park High School, all of whom have helped support and elevate me every day with their boundless creativity and sense of purpose. Thank you to Charlotte Brown-Nickson who guides our department with wisdom and grace. Thank you to my colleagues Michelle Yuson and Ayda Orozco - I feel lucky to count you as friends. Every day I learn from you and laugh with you, you help me see what's possible in the classroom.

This past fall I was lucky enough to travel to Paris as a guest of UNESCO and the Varkey Foundation to network with the best teachers from around the world. Thank you to the Society of the Sacred Hearts I met there: Manuel Chaves Quirós, Nicolas Gaube, Brendan Kenna, Mariette Wheeler, Ian Preston, Ana-Maria Rusu, Uroš Ocepek, and Lia Laela Sarah, among others. You inspire me with your brilliance.

Thank you to Jeff Anderson and Jennifer Shin of Audible, who marshaled an entire team of volunteers to help edit this project. I hope our partnership continues to bloom for years to come.

No book can ever be written without the support we get from loved ones. To everyone who loved a stranger until they felt like a friend: thank you. To everyone who has ever loved me: thank you more. To my friends and family Peter Geller, Kristen Masterson, Dan Helm, Joe Aponte, Barbara Kennedy, Ethan Crump, Jim Minardo, Francisco Garcia, Stephanie Ozaeta-Aponte, Wahab Ashraf, Tim Fleming, Cristiano Liborio, Mark Mager, Evan Bruno, Julianna Baldwin, Scott Homiak, Brad Sohn, Beth Adler-Duthe, Tenagne Girma-Jeffries, Alex Provda, Todd Gilchrist, Tony Teofilo, Matthew Adler, Jessica Berard, and Holly Russo today in particular. To my dad Neal Adler: the next book will be dedicated to you.

Finally, to the now tens of thousands of students over multiple books who have opened their hearts and trusted me to share their hurts and their pains and their dreams with the universe: You were never strangers, but simply angels in disguise. The world is yours. Go make it a good one.

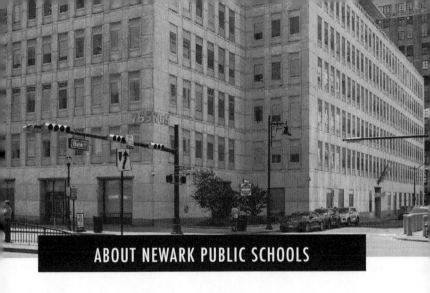

ABOUT NEWARK PUBLIC SCHOOLS

Dating back to 1676, Newark Public Schools is New Jersey's largest district, serving over 39,000 students in 63 schools, from pre-kindergarten through twelfth grade.

After more than two decades of state intervention, the district was returned to local control in 2018, and has since been guided by the leadership and vision of Superintendent Roger León, whose motto for 2023-2024 is it's a "Brand New Day," signifying the fresh perspective and innovative approaches Newark continues to bring to learning, and the transformative possibilities that await its students.

Five Newark schools, including two Newark high schools, have won the Blue Ribbon Award for academic excellence, the highest award given by the United States Department of Education.

NEWARK BOARD OF EDUCATION

The Newark Board of Education serves as a beacon of educational excellence in Essex County, dedicated to nurturing the potential of every student. With a commitment to innovation and inclusivity, the district continues to shape future generations and make a positive impact within its diverse, urban community.

NEWARK BOARD OF EDUCATION

S CIENCE PARK IS NEWARK's flagship high school, located in the University Heights section of the city and serving students in the seventh through twelfth grades with a rigorous curriculum centered on STEM learning. Routinely ranked among the top high schools in all of New Jersey, Science Park boasts a course selection that includes over 25 Advanced Placement classes as well as an International Baccalaureate Program, all designed to give each student opportunities at the highest possible level for interdisciplinary study, research, ethical leadership, and the development of an empathetic global perspective.

In 2009, Science Park High School was recognized by the US Department of Education as a Blue Ribbon School, the highest academic recognition in the country.

Under the guidance of longtime coach Jonathan Alston, the Science Park Debate Team has routinely ranked among the top programs in the country, boasting over 50 state champions and the United States National Debater of the Year in 2018.

NEWARK BOARD OF EDUCATION

Celebrating its 50th anniversary in 2024, Science Park High School is the premier academic institution in Newark, where big dreams meet proven results and children of all backgrounds are encouraged to take CHARGE of their future to create a better tomorrow.

S HAWN ADLER IS A first-generation German-American and a high school teacher of English at Science Park High School in Newark, New Jersey. He has edited five volumes of student memoirs: *The Class of COVID-19: Insights from the Inside*, *The Class of COVID-19: Second Wave*, *The Class of COVID-19: Unmasked*, *The Helpers*, and *We Were Strangers Once, Too*. These books have been featured on major news outlets like *NBC News*, *CNN*, *The Wall Street Journal*, and *People Magazine*, and have been celebrated at every level of American government, including by President Joe Biden. In 2023, Shawn was named a finalist for the Global Teacher Prize, a $1 million award of excellence called the "Nobel of Teaching." Shawn believes deeply that the people with the best stories live the best lives. He is proud to serve so many students by helping them find and tell theirs.

Made in United States
Troutdale, OR
11/28/2024

25410788R00149